BAKING FOR PROFIT

BAKING FOR PROFIT
Starting A Small Bakery

George Bathie

Edited by
Mike Battcock and Emma Judge

ITDG
PUBLISHING

Published by ITDG Publishing
103–105 Southampton Row, London WC1B 4HL, UK
www.itdgpublishing.org.uk

First published in 2000
Reprinted 2002

ISBN 1 85339 407 6

A catalogue record for this book is available from the British Library

ITDG Publishing is the publishing arm of the Intermediate Technology Development
Group. Our mission is to build the skills and capacity of people in developing
countries through the dissemination of information in all forms, enabling them to
improve the quality of their lives and that of future generations.

ITDG acknowledges the support of

NATIONAL
LOTTERY
CHARITIES
BOARD

Typeset by J&L Composition Ltd, Filey, North Yorkshire
Printed in Great Britain by SRP Limited, Exeter

Contents

Preface

This book is intended to help people establish a successful bakery business or improve an existing small bakery. In this book I have endeavoured to take the reader, step by step, through the stages of market research to establish evidence of a need for a bakery business in a particular location, and methods for determining the likelihood of success.

I would strongly recommend that any prospective entrepreneur should visit as many bakeries as possible (of all sizes, and not necessarily in the area where they hope to set up), studying what goes on and noting down the important facts of each stage of production. On a more personal level, anyone interested in setting up a small bakery needs to assess whether the prospect of earning a profit will be sufficiently rewarding to offset the hard work and often long, unsociable hours which can be the lot of the local baker.

George Bathie

Introduction

What is baking?

'To dry, harden or cook by the heat of the sun or fire; to make or cook in an oven; to become firm through heat.'

(*Chambers Concise Dictionary*)

The term baking is usually applied to flour-based foods (including all cereal products) for example, wheat, oats, maize and sorghum. These grains and flours have a relatively long shelf-life. Once they have been baked, goods such as breads and pastries have a shelf-life in the range of two to five days, whereas other goods (such as biscuits and some types of cake) have a shelf-life of several months as long as they have been correctly packaged.

The main purpose of baking is to change the eating quality of staple foodstuffs and to add variety to the diet. However, the baking process is also a preservation process. Baking exposes the product to high temperatures which will destroy most micro-organisms present in the product. (The soil bacteria *Bacillus subtilis mesintericus* is not destroyed by heat and can cause spoilage if the product is not stored correctly (as is discussed later on, in Chapter 6)). Contact with the hot air also reduces the moisture content at the surface of the baked product, thereby making it less suitable for bacteria to grow upon. The preservative action of baking is only effective after baking if the baked product is handled, packaged and stored correctly. Poorly stored products may become spoiled with moulds or bacteria.

During baking, food is heated by the hot air in the baking chamber (an oven) as well as by the heat of the floor, walls and trays of the chamber. Moisture at the surface of the food is evaporated by the hot air and, in larger products, such as bread and some biscuits, a dry crust is produced. Biscuit production uses slower heating which allows more moisture to escape from the surface of the food leaving a drier product, before it is sealed by the crust.

Baked goods are produced either from dough or batters, which are a mixture of flour and water made by mixing, beating, kneading or folding. The processing method will depend on the product being made and the ingredients being used.

Bread is either 'leavened' or 'unleavened'. Leavened bread is made from a mixture of flour, yeast, salt and water in measured quantities.

The mixture is left for a period of time at a certain temperature (21–29°C) to ferment and be brought to the correct condition from which good bread can be produced once it has been baked. Unleavened bread is made without yeast and so it is much quicker to process. As such bread is not fermented, the baked product is flat – hence its name.

Biscuits are the baked product of a mixture having not less than 8 per cent flour content and not more than 10 per cent moisture content after baking. Biscuits can be savoury, unsweetened or sweetened. They can be sandwiched with cream or iced after baking.

Cakes are made from a baked mixture of basic materials such as flour, fat, sugar, eggs and milk, with the addition of other optional ingredients such as fruit and nuts, etc.

The history of bread-making

Bread-making is one of the earliest food-processing technologies practised by man. It is known that more than 8000 years ago, in the Eastern Mediterranean and West Asia, people discovered that by deliberately planting wheat, the harvested grain could be stored until the next crop was ready to be harvested. This brought about a change in the pattern of life, enabling people to live in settlements and concentrate on growing more and better food.

Excavations of the oldest bakers' ovens in the world show that bread was known in Babylon in 4000 BC. It is not known when bread was first eaten in Egypt but the ancient Egyptians' custom of placing food in the tombs with the dead has proved that more than 5000 years ago, fermented bread was being made. Bread used to be baked in hot ashes or on heated stone slabs. Wedge-shaped bakers' ovens were being used from as early as 2500 BC with the bread being baked on the inner surface of these ovens. This method is still used in some parts of the Eastern Mediterranean today.

From Egypt, bread-making spread throughout the Mediterranean region, and in Greece, commercial bakeries were being established by the fifth century BC. The Romans developed large commercial bakeries in the second century BC to meet the demands of increasing bread consumption and they introduced bread-making to wherever they went in Europe and Africa. Until relatively recently, there had been very few changes in bread-making technologies apart from improvements in fermentation methods; the production of refined flours and the introduction of machinery to replace manual mixing and kneading. Over the last thirty years, the traditional processes have been revolutionized. However, traditional bread-making is still practised worldwide and is growing in popularity in many developing countries.

Principles of bread-making

The basic ingredients of leavened bread are flour (usually wheat flour), salt, water and yeast. Other ingredients can be added to change the flavour, appearance or keeping qualities of the bread. For example, fat or oil can be added to improve the flavour and to help slow down the staling process. Milk may be used instead of, or in combination with, water to produce a bread with a softer texture. Savoury ingredients such as cheese, fried onions, dried tomatoes or herbs may be added. Finally, sweet breads can be made by adding sugar, cinnamon and dried fruits to the basic dough.

A combination of different flours, such as rye, cassava, sorghum, millet or maize, mixed in varying proportions with wheat flour can be used to give a diverse range of breads based on the locally available staple. However, at least 70 per cent wheat needs to be used in a leavened bread to allow the bread to rise. Wheat flour has gradually become cheaper than the local staples and makes a superior quality bread, therefore it is bcoming less popular to produce breads from composite flours.

Unleavened breads are made from many different types of flour. These breads are popular across the world. Salt and water are added but no yeast is used. The flour and water mix is 'kneaded' to give a dough that is then baked. The resulting bread is flat, usually crisp and often hard. Chapatis, matzos and tortillas are all examples of unleavened bread.

Nutritional significance

Baked goods have a relatively high nutritional value, making them important in the diet. In common with other cereal products, they are good sources of energy, protein and some micro-nutrients, including iron, calcium and several B vitamins. The actual nutritional content of the flour depends upon the degree of milling. Traditional milling produces a flour that contains all of the crushed grain and thus has greater quantities of B vitamins, minerals and fibre in it. The texture of traditionally milled flours, however, is often coarse and the colour off-white. People's desire for whiter, less coarse flour has led millers to produce a flour where the bran is removed during the milling process. As many of the micro-nutrients are found in the bran, the nutritional content of these flours is much lower. In some parts of the world, other micro-nutrients are added to the flour in a process known as 'fortification'. If these flours are used in the baked goods, the nutritional quality of the product is even greater. Many baked products also contain added fats, sugar and sometimes fruits and nuts. These ingredients will increase the energy content of the products.

Opportunities in baking

The traditional process used to produce hand-made breads is suitable for small-scale production. The basic technologies are simple and small-scale production can be highly profitable, particularly when local cereals are used. Baked products are an ideal convenience food because they are not too expensive, they store relatively well, and they do not require any further processing before eating.

Baked goods provide plenty of scope for producers to use locally available ingredients in order to create a variety of value-added products. In general, it is more profitable to produce buns, biscuits and cakes than bread. However, prices for wheat flour vary from country to country and are heavily affected by price and import subsidies. Packaging requirements are often minimal as many of the products are for immediate consumption. This, therefore, reduces some of the problems for small-scale producers in terms of availability and access to packaging materials.

Chapter 1

First Steps – Feasibility and Business Planning

In order to set up a successful business, it is important to have an in-depth understanding of the local conditions and specific market demands. In this chapter we explain briefly how to collect and analyse this information.

Bakers usually have some basic ideas of the baked goods that they can produce and sell according to their own experience of where they live. Often their ideas come from seeing others successfully producing a specific product and then trying to copy them. However, when someone has an idea for a small business s/he will often try to start up straight away without having thought clearly about the different aspects involved in actually running the business. This hit or miss approach often results in failure during the first or second year of the business. To reduce this risk of failure it is necessary first to decide whether the idea is feasible (i.e. is it likely that the small business will be successful?). This involves carrying out a short market-survey and then usually requires the production of a feasibility study and possibly a business plan. A feasibility study is a good way of working out the likely success of a business on paper before scarce resources are spent in actually getting started.

Feasibility study

The entrepreneur has to find out whether s/he is capable of producing the food in the required amounts and at the correct quality and price. It is also necessary to source the equipment, raw materials and packaging to make the food in the required amounts. A labour force may need to be trained and finance obtained. Finding out about all these things is known as carrying out a feasibility study.

The general procedure for conducting feasibility studies is to:

1 gather information
2 analyse and interpret the information
3 use the analysis to plan the business.

The feasibility study has three components:

o marketing aspects: establishing the demand for the food, finding out how much to make each day, and considering how to promote and sell the food
o technical aspects: including identifying premises, selecting equipment and raw materials, and thinking about the quality control and packaging needed to produce this amount of food
o financial and legal aspects: investigating loans or finance needed to support this level of production, and finding out about business registration, certificates, and financial arrangements with suppliers and customers.

A feasibility study gives the entrepreneur the opportunity to think through what the business will involve in practice and to identify likely problems, as well as giving him/her the confidence to go ahead – see Box 1.

Box 1 The three stages of a feasibility study

1st stage – Market feasibility

- Market research
- Selling strategy
- Expected market size/share
- Competitors

2nd stage – Technical feasibility

- Scale of production needed to meet market-share
- Equipment, materials, services and labour needed for scale of production selected
- Quality control
- Distribution

3rd stage – Financial feasibility

- Start-up costs
- Cashflow for one year (income and expenditure)
- Loan required
- Business development over three years
- Profitability/sustainability
- Making a decision

When the results of the study have been organized and written down, they can be used to draw up a business plan. If a loan is needed, the funding agency or bank will usually need such a simple business plan to show that the entrepreneur is serious about the work and has thought about likely problems. This gives the funders more confidence that their loan will be repaid.

The business plan has the following three functions.

o It is the basis of a loan request.
o It shows that the entrepreneur has thought seriously about the business and how it will develop.
o It is a working tool to help the entrepreneur plan for the future. We will now look at each of these three stages in more detail.

Gathering information

Start with the customer

Assuming that the entrepreneur has an idea for a product, the first thing to do is to find out from potential customers what level of demand there is for the baked goods (or what is 'the market' for the food). A simple market-survey should be carried out by talking to people who are expected to buy the product. Ask them how much they will buy how often and for what price. The market study should be a short exercise so as to keep the costs low. In-depth market research is not necessary in most situations. Using the information gathered from potential customers, the entrepreneur can then work out the total demand for the product. This involves asking a number of questions such as:

o are the people interviewed really representative of all potential customers?
o how many potential customers are there in total?
o will people in different income groups buy different amounts of food or at different frequencies?

It might be helpful to ask potential customers about where they buy baked goods at present, what packaging they prefer, what is good or bad about the quality of the baked goods they buy and what they would like to change. The entrepreneur also needs to think about how the baked goods are actually going to be sold and what any competitors are doing. This is the next stage in determining the market.

Statistical figures

Helpful, basic information is usually obtainable from government statistical offices, for example:

o the population and the breakdown of these figures at the last census, with the figures split up into adult males and adult females, and further subdivided into married and single groups, with younger people subdivided into gender and age groups. If possible, brief information giving a reasonable estimate of population growth from the date of the last census would be useful to obtain because it would provide a reasonably accurate update on the original information

o any details available on the estimated per capita earning power
o any details available on local employment/unemployment figures, if possible, split into various categories.

Competitors

Being knowledgeable about the existence and nature of any competition is critical to the success of any business. The entrepreneur should therefore find out the answers to the following questions.

o Who is producing similar products?
o Where are they located?
o What is the quality and price of their products?
o What offers or incentives do they give to retailers?
o What can the entrepreneur do to make the new product better?
o Why would a customer change to buy the new product?
o What are competitors likely to do if a new product is introduced?

As much information as possible should also be obtained on the quantity of purchases by caterers, hoteliers and food retailers per day. Flour suppliers may give information of the amount of bags (baggage) supplied to a potential customer. The entrepreneur should draw up a large, detailed map of the area with plotted sites of all the bakeries, and other potential competitors, with delivery routes (if they exist) marked in different colours, including bakery goods being delivered into the area from outside. This will highlight the extent and coverage of the competition.

Information should be obtained about the preferred size and shape of loaves, and their baked weight. The study should also seek to give reasons supporting their choice of size and shape based on observation and experience of local markets.

The entrepreneur then needs to decide how much of the estimated demand can be met by their proposed production. The percentage of total demand that can be met by new businesses, depends on the number and size of competitors.

In summary, the entrepreneur can use all this information to decide which food to make, how much food s/he will have to make each week to meet a known share of the total demand and where there is a chance of competing against other producers. The main questions are: 'Is it a good idea?' and 'Shall I go ahead and invest in the business?'.

A note about new products

There are obvious advantages in making a product that is new to an area (for example, there will be no competitors initially). However, the entrepreneur should be very sure that people will buy the new food at the expected price. This requires a trial production to make samples for test-marketing (for potential customers to taste the food and give their opinion). All of this takes longer, and costs more, than making products that are already known. In addition, up to 80 per cent of new products fail within the first year, so the risks are higher and obtaining a loan may be more difficult. A good compromise is often found by modifying an existing product to create something different that would appeal to a new market.

Location

The site of the new bakery is also significant in the feasibility study. If the bakery is intended to serve an urban area, then the likelihood is that a large number of the population will eat bread and other bakery products to some degree, depending upon their means. Whereas, if the intention is to serve and develop a rural area, there may be a number of people who only eat the food that they grow for their own consumption and therefore, may have little need for bread and other bakery products.

The feasibility study for the site of the bakery and area chosen should also include an outline of any construction work needed (or any modification required should the project be an existing operation) together with the planned date of completion for the construction work.

Costs

Clearly it is important to calculate the likely cost of setting up and running the bakery. The setting-up costs will include the cost of any construction work to the buildings, and the cost of purchasing the bakery equipment. Once the bakery is operating, there will be costs associated with running the equipment, particularly the ovens, and with employing staff.

Construction work

The feasibility study will have identified any building work that may need to be carried out and the labour and material costs for this need to be worked out. In some countries, it is necessary to obtain planning approval from the local authority before the building work can go ahead, and there is usually a charge for such an application for approval.

Equipment purchase

There is a wide range of equipment that can be purchased for use in a bakery (see Chapter 3), some of which is essential to the operation. The price of the equipment can vary considerably between suppliers, and so it would be wise to obtain several quotes for each piece of equipment to be purchased.

Operating the equipment

With any type of oven, the actual baking costs of the oven per hour can be worked out to a reasonably accurate figure by dividing the total baking time into the cost of fuel (i.e. wood, oil, etc.). While an oven is rising in temperature to the desired baking temperature for bread, it should be possible to bake some smaller items and again at the end of the bread baking (during the period of dropping temperature when the oven is switched off or the fire drawn out). The total baking period will include the time taken to bake the smaller items in the calculation. The result should be a full deck cost per hour or a full oven cost per hour, from which reasonably accurate batch-baking costs can be calculated for costing purposes.

Employees

Setting up and running a small bakery means that several roles have to be fulfilled. Future expansion might mean that later on some of the responsibilities can be handed over, but to begin with, a realistic and affordable staffing level must be calculated.

Basically, the tasks involved in running a small-scale bakery involve the following:

- ○ market research
- ○ purchase of raw ingredients
- ○ cleaning and maintenance of the equipment and the production place
- ○ production of the baked goods
- ○ advertising and marketing of the finished goods
- ○ financial management and account keeping.

At the smallest scale, these tasks can be completed by one person, although it would be very time consuming. It is probably advisable to employ extra staff to help with the cleaning and marketing of the products.

It is preferable that the person responsible for baking the goods has some training or previous experience in this art. Training courses on bread-making are available in many countries and once the basic skills have been learned, they can quickly be adapted to include a range of products.

Analysis and interpretation of data

Having collected the statistical and commercial information, the next step is to correlate all this into a clear format that will make the basis for a business plan (projection). An example of the types of categories you would need to use for the data now follows.

Box 2 Example calculations for projecting demand for bread in a sample population

- the area population of 100,000 people (which includes all ages, etc.)
- the annual population growth (e.g. estimated at 2 per cent)
- the unit of bread used in the calculation (e.g. 450g)
- the estimated averages of daily eating habits (of bread), e.g.
  - 10 per cent of the population eat no bread in their diet, but subsist on their own home grown crops and livestock.
  - 40 per cent of the population eat a lot of bread daily, estimated at 450g average per person per day. Fifty per cent of the population eat half this amount daily, estimated at 225g average per person per day.

The projections set out in Table 1 are for illustration purposes only, but if the figures were factual, all that would be required would be to extend into the 'cash value' column to complete the picture.

If the figures that have been projected indicate that there is a reasonable market for bread, then the feasibility study should be continued, listing comments about any business that has already been promised. Reasoned opinions about the initial start-up and production throughput on one shift of eight hours' duration, expressed in units per hour, should be given. Also, the revised throughput per hour once the production team has settled in, after perhaps four to six months of working together, should be forecast.

If the figures that have been entered into the projection indicate little hope of the bakery venture becoming successful, then you must reconsider the project.

Table 1 Projected demand for bread in the area (extended for five years)

Year	Estimated population	90 per cent	40 per cent (450g)	50 per cent (225g)	Total in units of 450g	Cash value
Start	100,000	90,000	40,000	50,000	65,000	
One	102,000	91,800	40,800	51,000	66,300	
Two	104,040	93,636	41,616	52,020	67,626	
Three	106,120	95,508	42,448	53,060	68,978	
Four	108,243	97,418	43,297	54,121	70,358	
Five	110,407	99,366	44,163	55,203	71,765	

Using the analysis to plan the business

Having established that there is a potential market for more bakery products and having established access to the necessary finance/loans/ credit and potential premises from which to operate, the entrepreneur should now complete a production plan and think about the set-up for the bakery operation.

As mentioned, a feasibility study requires an estimation of the capital outlay likely to be involved in setting up a baking operation. A plan layout should be chosen that is suited to the area for which the operation is being planned. The following suggested plan layouts include one for an operation using no mechanical machinery in the production operation (Figure 1.1) and two others for bakeries which are mechanically equipped to differing levels of production throughput (Figures 1.2 and 1.3). Each plan has an accompanying list of items required such as furniture, oven or ovens, mechanical equipment. Lists are also given of smaller items, for example bread tins, baking trays, cake hoops, small tins and hand tools.

Cost analysis

At an early stage in the process of forming an operation, the habit of careful costing should be started with regard to all proposed activities of the bakery, including start-up and running costs associated with the buildings, machinery and equipment, furnishing, vehicles, the various production processes and staffing costs. Documents concerning the following need to be prepared:

- loan and working capital
- project cost
- salaries and wages

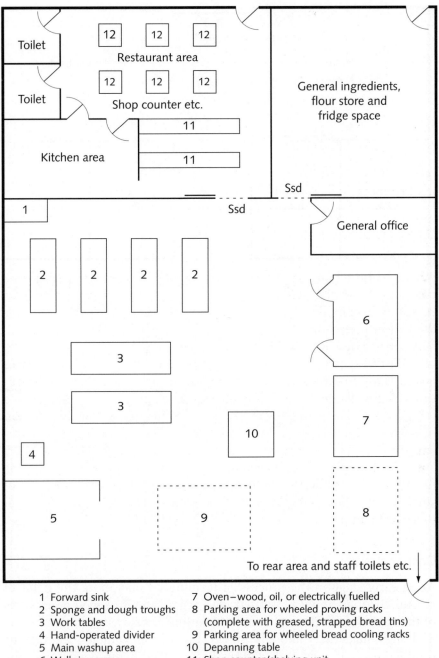

1 Forward sink
2 Sponge and dough troughs
3 Work tables
4 Hand-operated divider
5 Main washup area
6 Walk-in prover
7 Oven–wood, oil, or electrically fuelled
8 Parking area for wheeled proving racks
   (complete with greased, strapped bread tins)
9 Parking area for wheeled bread cooling racks
10 Depanning table
11 Shop counter/shelving unit
12 Restaurant tables

Fire precautions: Hydrants, hoses, fire buckets, and appliances to be sited in accordance with local regulations. Ssd = sliding security door

Figure 1.1: Small hand-operated bakery with retail shop and restaurant
(not to scale)

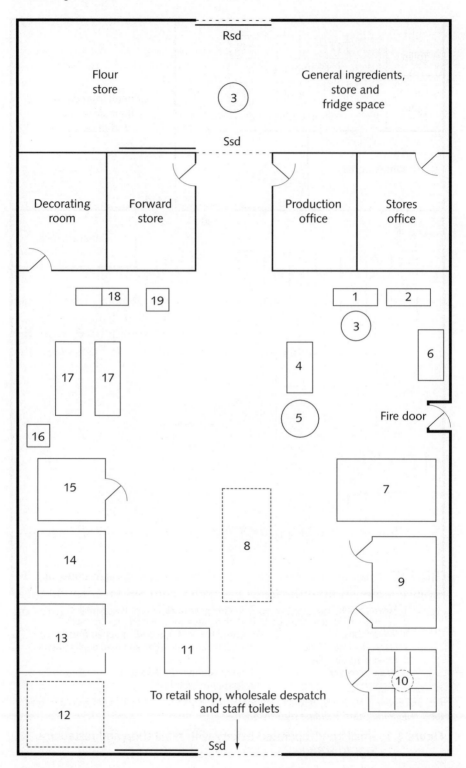

1 Dough mixer
2 Water meter/tempering tank
3 Dough mixing bowls
4 Mechanical dough divider
5 Conical moulder (umbrella)
6 Forward sink
7 Large bread moulding table
   (moulding by hand)
8 Parking area for wheeled proving racks
   (complete with greased, strapped
   bread tins)

9 Walk-in prover
10 Rack oven (four seater)
11 Depanning table
12 Parking area for wheeled bread cooling racks
13 Main washup area
14 Confectionery oven (two deck)
15 Final prover for confectionery oven
16 Hand-operated dough divider
17 Confectionery department work tables
18 Mechanical dough brake
19 Upright variable mixer

Fire precautions: Hydrants, hoses, fire buckets, and appliances to be sited in accordance with local fire regulations. Ssd = sliding security door, Rsd = roller security door

Figure 1.2: Small partly-mechanized bakery with retail shop and wholesale despatch *(not to scale)*

o a projected profit and loss account
o a forward cash-flow projection over a period to be decided.

The production of a range of products for, perhaps, the first six months of operation should be costed, including calculations for recipes at actual cost for the ingredients and wrapping used. Notional pro rata cost figures should also be worked out in respect of the following:

o direct cost of production
   o management and labour
   o fuel, electricity and water
o indirect cost of production
   o administration and general expenses
   o advertising and selling costs
   o depreciation
   o loan repayments
   o financial charges including other preliminary and unforeseen expenses.

Once the production has started, the pro rata figures should be reviewed in relation to the items listed above under direct and indirect costs, when the bakery manager is in a position to produce figures on production timings.

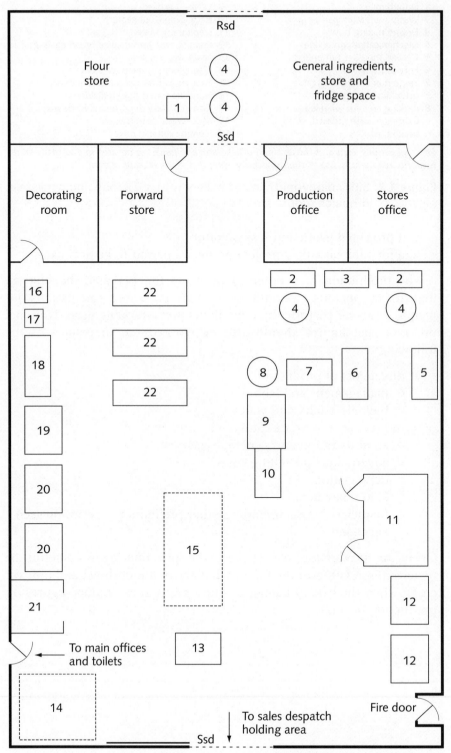

1 Mechanical flour sifter (can be wheeled out into baking hall if required)	12 Rack ovens (four seaters)
2 Dough mixers	13 Depanning table
3 Water meter/tempering tank	14 Parking area for wheeled bread cooling rack
4 Dough mixing bowls	15 Parking area for wheeled proving racks (complete with greased, strapped bread tins
5 Forward washup sink	16 Upright variable mixer
6 Mixing bowl hoist	17 Hand-operated dough divider
7 Mechanical dough divider	18 Mechanical dough brake
8 Conical moulder (umbrella)	19 Final prover for confectionery ovens
9 Interim prover	20 Confectionery ovens
10 Final moulder	21 Main washup area
11 Walk-in final prover	22 Confectionery department work tables

Fire precautions: Hydrants, hoses, fire buckets, and appliances to be sited in accordance with local fire regulations. Ssd = sliding security door, Rsd = roller security door

Figure 1.3: Medium-sized semi-automatic bakery *(not to scale)*

Chapter 2
Setting Up The Bakery

Location

When setting up a bakery it is essential that the condition of the building, the materials of construction and its position are all suitable for food production – and, indeed, this is often a legal requirement. A bakery plant should not be located near swamps, ditches, refuse dumps or other places where insects and rodents are likely to be found in large numbers. The site should be cleared of undergrowth and kept clean of debris and waste food that could attract rodents and flies. The site should also allow waste water to drain away freely and have suitable facilities for removing or disposing of waste food and rubbish away from the site. A supply of clean water is also essential.

Layout of the building and general hygiene

Ideally, the operational areas of the bakery building should be at ground-floor level throughout, with the raw materials/ingredients entering at one end and eventually leaving the despatch area as finished products. Within reason, the various operations being used in a plant should be kept separate in order to prevent contamination – for example perishable raw materials should be kept separately from non-perishable raw materials. Packaging material should also be separately stored and, if there are plans for a main office, it should be sited within the building but away from the other areas. Toilets, if at all possible, should be housed in a separate building. If they have to be placed in the main building, there should be two doors between the WC and the production area. For good hygiene, workers must have access to hand-washing facilities with soap and clean towels.

It's very important that thought be given to any possible future expansion so that when the time comes, little structural alteration, if any, will be required. Space should also be available around certain points outside the building for the erection or sinking of fuel tanks.

Figure 2.1 shows a typical layout of a food processing room, showing how raw materials move through the process, and the room, without paths crossing.

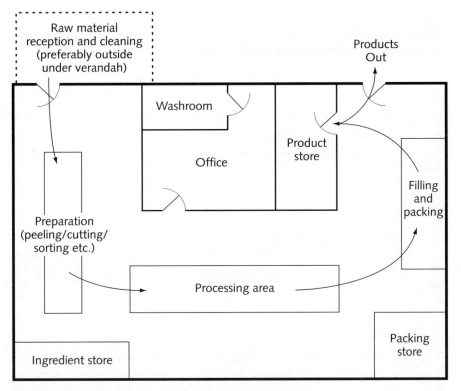

Figure 2.1: Typical layout of food-processing room

Walls and general internal finish

Attention should be given to preventing the access of birds, rodents and flying insects through gaps in the roof structure and, in particular, where the roof joins the wall. In tropical climates, overhanging roofs that keep the direct sunlight from the building walls will make life for the workers more comfortable.

All internal walls should be (at least) smooth-plastered in production areas to allow for thorough cleaning. Ledges and rough finishes accumulate dust and are difficult to clean. Selected areas, for example, behind sinks or where machinery will cause considerable splashing, should be ceramic tiled.

The floor

The floor should be made of good quality concrete and should slope to a central drainage channel so that at the end of the day the whole area can be hosed down and drained naturally. The drainage channel should be fitted with a heavy iron grating that can be easily removed for internal cleaning of the drain. Wire mesh should be fitted at the end of the drain where it exits from the building, as an open drain at this point provides a corridor for rodents to enter the premises.

Lighting

Good lighting for general work can be provided by fluorescent tubes. If machinery with fast-moving exposed parts (such as mills) are being used, it is important for safety reasons to also have normal incandescent lighting.

Electricity

In view of the fact that the plant is likely to need hosing down, any electric points should be placed at high levels. Ideally, waterproof outlets should be used but in many cases due to their high cost this will not prove possible.

Water supply

There should always be an adequate and continuous supply of clean water available. A good flow of cold water and an adequate supply of hot is required. Unless great reliance can be placed upon the mains supply, a high-level water-storage tank would prove extremely useful. It should be covered with a close-fitting, lidded arrangement and should be regularly inspected for any evidence of contamination build-up (from flour dust and dirt).

Ventilation

Good ventilation is essential where heating operations are taking place. Large window openings covered with mesh allow natural light and air to enter the building while preventing insects and birds from coming in. If affordable, electric fans fitted on the ceilings are recommended as well.

Chapter 3
Equipment

How to select equipment

Buying bakery equipment requires considerable and careful thought in deciding what is best for the individual's specific needs. It is a good idea for prospective buyers to visit trade fairs, manufacturers, workshops and equipment retailers where bakery equipment is on display, or to visit operating bakeries where certain kinds of equipment can be seen in action. Expert opinions should be sought whenever possible. When considering the suitability of the equipment, some important factors should be taken into account:

○ the robustness of the equipment
○ the simplicity of servicing, cleaning and maintenance
○ whether the equipment can be repaired locally
○ what spares must be held
○ how long it will take to get replacement parts.

Types of equipment

There are many different pieces and types of equipment available to the baker. Some of these are essential to the bakery operation (for example, ovens) whilst others simply provide optional benefits (for example, labour-saving devices and equipment that increase the speed of production). It is important to think carefully about what pieces of equipment are essential to the bakery operation being planned, and which, if any, of the additional pieces of equipment will be of benefit. The following list of bakery equipment is intended simply as a guide to the equipment available and not as a list of equipment that must be purchased.

Ovens

The type of oven, or ovens, required depends very much on the size and type of the operation being planned. Bread is normally the larger part of any bakery's production throughput, although there are certain other non-fermented products which can be baked off in the same temperature range as fermented products. (These can either be baked along with fermented products or in alternate batches with bread thus enabling production of a range of products). While estimates of the cost of running the ovens can be obtained from the oven manufacturers, the actual costs depend more upon a number of things such as:

○ how efficiently the oven space is kept used with products being baked. Unused oven space becomes an 'on cost' to the operation

○ the fact that the throughput of products in the independently heat-controlled oven decks will go more smoothly on 'dropping heat', with the last batch being, for example, meringues which can dry out with the heat switched off and the deck door left open

○ the fact that with the extended shelf-life that certain cakes, biscuits, etc. possess, efficient baking production can be planned so that longer production runs can be carried out on specific days, leading to a smoother throughput with less danger of over-baking particular products. Practice will increase efficiency.

The oven capacity of any bakery controls the production volume of oven-baked products. It is therefore *very* important to become aware of the versatility of the types of ovens under consideration and to determine their suitability to the bakery's present and future needs. There now follows a description of some of the better known types of oven that are suitable for small-scale use in tropical conditions.

Beehive oven

The principle of operation in these ovens is simple: build a fire in a massive dome, let it burn until the walls are sufficiently hot, then remove the fire and bake using the heat retained in the structure of the oven. These ovens are called retained-heat ovens because they do not directly use the fire for baking but, instead, use the heat retained in the oven walls. They are usually built of fired brick or clay, over an open hearth with an opening at the front, in the shape of a beehive or dome with a square base and a blunt point at the top.

Once the embers have been cleared out, the hearth is swabbed out with a wet rag before the loaves are put inside to be baked and this cools the surface and increases the humidity of the baking atmosphere. Some skill and experience is needed to judge the correct temperature at which to remove the embers and put the bread in. Capacity is limited by the size of the hearth and the heat-retention properties of the walls. These ovens are suitable for domestic use or small-scale bakeries.

Improved Ghanaian baking oven

This oven designed by the University of Ghana is based on the traditional direct-fired dome-shaped oven. It is built with fired clay bricks held together with clay containing salt. The base of the oven is filled with broken glass and salt-containing clay to improve heat retention. It is completed with a layer of fired bricks and a covering of clay to form the floor of the oven. The outside of the oven is coated in a thin layer of clay and the opening is covered by a hard wood door. During baking this is covered with a moistened sack to prevent charring and to make a good seal.

Labour requirements are estimated at about three days for one person, and materials should be available locally. The inclusion of a shelf doubles the capacity of the oven and saves time and fuel. The capacity of the oven is about 100 × 500g (1lb) loaves, with a baking time of between 20 and 25 minutes, which means it is sufficient for a small-scale business operation.

Double oil-drum oven

This is a simple indirect-fired oven. It consists of a baking cavity made from two oil-drums, one pushed inside the other, set over a fire box. A chimney is inserted into the top of the drums which are enclosed in a box filled with dirt to insulate the oven. The original design uses corrugated iron to make the fire box but brick may be used instead. It is also suggested that about 15cm (6″) of loose sand is placed in the base of the oven to distribute the heat evenly and prevent burning of the bread.

This oven is relatively inexpensive and quick to build (about 16 man hours), requiring few constructional skills and tools. It heats up quickly but capacity is limited to 10–12 × 500g (1lb) loaves.

Oil-drum and brick oven

This oven was designed to enable village bakeries to be set up at relatively low cost. It consists of a fire box formed from a brick wall built on top of a concrete base with a gap at one end for the stoke-hole. Two steel plates and steel bars act as the bases and supports for the two ovens made from one 200-litre oil-drum cut in half. Larger four-oven constructions are possible to make using two oil-drums instead of one.

Simple masonry and welding skills and approximately 18 man hours are needed for construction of this oven and the materials should be readily available in most villages. Capacity is about 18–24 × 500g (1lb) loaves and baking time is about 20 minutes. The oven takes about three hours to heat up, and if double ovens are used the output would be sufficient to meet the requirements of a village bakery. Baked goods other than bread can be cooked when bread-baking is finished and the oven is cooling down.

Tandoor oven

A typical tandoor oven uses either wood or charcoal as fuel. The oven is built with a fired ceramic liner which is porous due to a high straw content in the original clay body. The liner is then packed in mud, sand or cement. At the bottom of the oven, there is an air inlet and some-times a grate to promote complete and even combustion. The fire burns in the same chamber as the food bakes and at the same time. After the oven has heated up, flattened discs of dough are slapped onto the inner walls of the oven.

The band-travelling oven

The products are fed in at one end of the oven, passing through the heated portion on a moving belt and extracted from the other end, having been baked at varying controlled speeds. These ovens are supplied in various sizes and are probably most appropriate for semi-automatic plants. The more expensive oven of this type can be linked into a fully automatic plant. Tunnel ovens are suitable for long baking runs of bread-type products and perform very well when they are kept continuously full. This oven is not suitable for 'mixed' bakes, i.e. prod-ucts of differing sizes and weights, and is not generally appropriate for small-scale use.

The swing-tray oven

This is another type of travelling oven which operates with the products being fed in on broad swinging trays, taking three to four baking trays each and travelling a fixed route inside the oven. The prod-ucts eventually emerge from the same opening they were initially fed into. Like the tunnel oven, the swing-tray oven operates at varying con-trolled speeds and temperatures. With the feeding and extraction at the same point, there can be a saving in labour costs.

The rack oven

This oven has quite a simple design and it takes up limited floor space, depending on size. It is versatile and can bake a variety of items requir-ing the same level of baking temperature. This type of oven can be supplied with up to eight racks, the principle being that the racks are wheeled into the oven onto a revolving floor and the products bake evenly as the floor and racks revolve. Hot air is distributed over and under each baking tray to ensure the uniform baking of the products. Full details about the functioning of rack ovens is freely available from the manufacturers. The shelf runners of the racks can be positioned to allow about 40mm clearance between the top of the baked product and the underside of the tray immediately above, i.e. eight pairs of shelf runners per rack for tinned bread – which for dual-purpose racks can be increased to sixteen pairs of runners to accommodate either bread or rolls or buns, etc., or eighteen pairs of runners for the small items alone. With tinned bread, it is usual to slide in three straps of four loaves per relative shelf-fitting, making 96 loaves per filled rack.

Multi-deck electric ovens

Each deck can accommodate three baking trays 30″ × 18″ (approximately 67.5 × 45.75cm) and each deck is independently heated with top and bottom heat-controls and overriding thermostats. The crown heights can be variable from 150mm for small items to 250mm for high-domed types of bread. The multi-decks can be all high-crown or all low-crown ovens, or a mixture of high and low, but the requirement of 'working height' may limit the number of decks. These are independent of each other and contribute to a wide variety being baked at the same time. Single-deck ovens are available.

Peel ovens

This refers to any oven that requires the use of an oven peel to load or offload baking trays of products. Fuelling can be by oil or electricity, or, in the instance of homemade ovens, by burning wood in the baking chamber. These ovens can be quite effective but are not as versatile as the small multi-decked type. Suitable products are those requiring high-temperature baking and products being baked at lower temperatures that require time for the oven to cool.

Other equipment

Flour sifter/sieve

This is a utensil with a mesh of wire or nylon, etc. through which dry materials may be passed to remove large particles or foreign matter. Although a flour sifter is often viewed as an optional piece of equipment, it is a very necessary piece of equipment where hygiene regulations are strictly controlled and applied. The type which can double up as a 'crumber' can prove to be an asset.

Dough mixer

This is a machine which mechanically mixes the ingredients of a recipe. A robust, conventional type of single-arm, two-speed mixer with a bowl guard and moveable mixing bowl, plus two spare bowls, is recommended. A model with an hermetically sealed motor with automatic lubrication is dustproof and easy to keep clean, requiring only that a specific oil level be maintained. Mixing machines are manufactured in different sizes and allowance should be made for production-volume expansion when deciding upon the size of machine.

Bowl hoist

This is often viewed as an optional piece of equipment which is provided to lift the mixing bowl and dough up to the dough-divider hopper and refill the dough hopper. The advantages of the bowl hoist is that it is both labour-saving and also removes the danger of knives scratching the inside of the mixing bowl if the dough is removed and put into the divider hopper by hand.

Hand divider

This piece of equipment is useful for the small- to medium-size bakery considering making small bread buns. A hand-operated bun/roll divider can cut 36 pieces of dough of equal weight up to a range of 115g each. The divider head can be bolted to a table or fixed on to a moveable stand. Each machine is supplied with a steel cutting-pan and, in order to enhance the production throughput, the buyer is recommended to acquire two spare pans.

This type of machine is very simple to operate and can be easily cleaned. If it is mounted on a stand it can be easily shifted out of the way when not in use.

Dough divider

This will automatically divide the bulk dough in the hopper into equal pieces using the principle of a mechanical suction arrangement. This type of machine can cut on a range as low as 200–250g and up to around 2000–2200g, at an hourly rate of between 750 and 1800 pieces. This can be further enhanced by fixing a splitter board to the final moulder. However, whichever divider is preferred, particular care should be taken over the matter of the manufacturer's instructions in cleaning the dividing parts of the machine and in the use of edible oil on the knife blade. (This may be required after washing to prevent the blade rusting.) This eases the bulk dough down into the hopper.

Conical ball moulder

Often known as the 'umbrella' moulder, this machine very quickly moulds the cut dough piece into a ball shape and passes it on to the interim prover (see below). The dough piece is balled up manually on a table and set aside in close lines under a cloth to prevent 'skinning', or in a special drawer cabinet to rest for the required time before being given a final hand mould and placed into bread tins ready for final proof. The umbrella moulder and the interim prover combine to per-form this function mechanically.

The dough piece from the divider drops on to the umbrella moulder and is led right around the outside of the cone by enclosing sleeves and then moulded into a ball. Finally, the ball-shaped piece of dough drops, via a chute, into a moving pocket where it passes around the interim prover at a pre-set speed.

While the dough piece is travelling around the cone of the umbrella moulder, it passes under a hot or cold blower to form a very thin skin aimed at preventing the dough sticking to the cone. The dough piece can also, if necessary, be lightly flour-dusted by a mechanically operated duster.

The umbrella moulder operates at a fixed speed, spinning fast enough to allow the dough piece to pass quickly round the cone from the divider to the interim prover.

Interim prover

This is a cabinet in which steam and heat can be applied and in which fermented goods are proved prior to baking. The main purpose of the interim or first prover is to temporarily rest the dough pieces which have been ball-moulded in the umbrella moulder. The dough balls pass through the prover for a predetermined period, depending upon their size, so that the dough pieces have 'recovered' before being dropped into the hopper of the final moulder. The throughput times can be adjusted as appropriate to 9, 12 or 16 minutes.

These provers can be supplied in varying shapes and sizes to suit buyer's specific productions needs. They are fitted with temperature and humidity controls and ultraviolet lights to help contain the development of mould and bacteria within the prover. A steaming device (aimed at keeping the humidity within the prover under strict control) is also available as an extra.

Final moulder

The function of this machine is to give a final mould to the dough piece before it is placed on to a tray or into tins. The principle is that the rested dough piece drops from the interim prover exit-chute into the moulder hopper, down through sheeting rollers and is curled up like a swiss roll under a strip of chain mesh. It then continues along a conveyor belt under an adjustable pressure plate that runs the moulded loaf out of the other end ready for tinning. Alternatively, the curled sheeted dough piece can run through under a pressure plate with a splitting attachment that will divide the moulded dough piece into two or four pieces.

When the moulded loaves have been trayed or tinned, they are then racked and pushed into a 'wheel in' final prover.

Final prover
The size of the final prover depends upon the volume of production passing through it. For production up to and including the level of semi-automatic equipment, the wheel-in type of final prover is suitable. This is basically a chamber into which racks of fermented products can be wheeled to rest until the products have risen to a required volume height before being baked. They can vary in size depending upon the production-volume. The chamber can be large enough to house numerous racks that are wheeled in at one end and extracted from the other. The oven operator will be continuously moving the racks forward towards the exit doors as required.

The prover can also have a smaller capacity, with the racks being wheeled in and out of the same opening. Irrespective of its size or whether it is factory made or locally built, the final prover must be fitted with a heating and steaming unit capable of achieving a proving chamber temperature level of between 35°C and 43°C, with a humidity level of around 85 per cent.

There are also temporary 'tented' structures that can be erected with a light framework and enclosed in heavy-duty plastic sheeting or light canvas, into which steam can be introduced. A simple arrangement using a frequently topped-up pan of water boiling on a small fire produces sufficient steam to prevent dough surfaces skinning. This arrangement is not suitable for serious inclusion in a feasibility study and it tends to slow down the rate of fermentation in the final stage.

Note: Special care must be taken to ensure that excessive steaming is not given to the products, and that they are not allowed to become wet, or proven beyond the optimum period from which good results can be obtained. If this is allowed to happen there may be a danger of the unbaked loaf collapsing as it is being put into the oven, owing to the upper structure being weakened.

Upright planetary mixer
The ingredients of a recipe are mechanically mixed by a vertical machine. This mixer is essential for any bakery that produces cake batters, whisks creams, and egg whites, etc., or makes small confectionery, fermented doughs or other types of doughs.

These machines are supplied in various sizes, ranging from the table model to the large floor-based machines with as much as 150-litre bowl capacity. Most machines are supplied with two detachable bowls of different capacity. Each bowl has its own whisk, beater and dough hook. The older design machines usually operate on four speeds, regulated by a side gear change for which the machine has to be in the 'stopped' position. The more modern machines are fitted with a variable mixing-speed arrangement that is increased or decreased by the gradual movement of a side lever and requires no actual gear change.

Pastry brake
This machine can be either mechanically or hand-operated and is used for rolling or pinning out pastry and dough into sheets of a specific thickness by gradual reduction. The dough is passed back and forth through two revolving rollers until the desired sheet thickness has been obtained.

The pastry brake is a set of two equal-sized, smooth-surfaced rollers which adjoin a flat steel platform table arrangement on either side. A hand guard is fitted over the rollers which can slant forwards or backwards and at the same time change the direction of the rollers – and protect the operator's hands from getting too near the rollers pulling the sheet of pastry through. The hand-operated pastry brake operates on the same principle.

One advantage of this machine is its ability, when adjusted to the desired setting, to produce exactly the same dough-sheet thickness as often as is required, day after day – which is a positive support to the maintenance of costing calculations and quality control.

Biscuit maker
Hand-made biscuits can be a very profitable sideline for the small- to medium-sized bakery. For the cut-out type of biscuit, the pastry brake is a useful aid for boosting production. The hand-operated divider is also useful for biscuits of a type that require the dough to be divided into pieces of equal weight, rolled into balls and flattened or given a slight pinning before traying up.

Machinery manufacturers now offer a small biscuit unit with interchangeable indented roller moulds that operate quite successfully once the baker has the right consistency for shortbread and shortcake doughs and has mastered the technique of feeding the doughs onto the machine. The manufacturers claim an approximate product capacity of around 200kg per hour. This may be a good investment if biscuits of this type are to be included in the regular throughput.

Generator
In circumstances where the mains supply of electricity may be erratic, expensive, or non existent, advice should be sought about other

available back-up facilities. Expert opinion should be sought on the suitability of the bakery having its own generator, or of having a solar-heating panel on the roof for a supply of hot water, and/or a boiler unit for the supply of hot water or steam.

Work tables
These may be fitted with or without under-shelving. They should preferably be made of wood.

Other small equipment
In addition to the larger equipment already mentioned, there are various items that will also be required in the bakery in numbers related to the proposed size of the operation. These are:

- **glaze brushes**, which are used to give a glossy surface to the product
- **table-sweeping brushes**, which are used for keeping the working area clean
- **hard floor-brushes, soft floor-brushes** and **floor-scrubbing brushes** – all of which are used for keeping the working area clean
- **nail brushes**, which are used for keeping the hands of operators clean
- **table-dusting boxes**, which are used to shake a thin layer of flour onto the table for kneading
- **plastic two-gallon buckets and basins**, which are used as containers for mixing ingredients
- two **dipping forks**, which are needed for decorating cakes
- two **dough dockers**, which are utensils consisting of a number of spikes that are used for puncturing the surface of dough or pastry
- one set of **expanding markers**
- a fully stocked **first-aid box**
- one **funnel**, which is used to transfer liquids from one container to another
- various **hand whisks**, which are bundles of wires arranged so that they may be handled and used as a beater
- two sets of **knives** – one set of cutting knives and one set of palette knives
- **liquid measurers**, which are used for measuring the correct amount of water for dough, etc.
- **oven gloves**, which are used to protect the hands of operators
- an **oven peel**, which is a flat shovel made of wood or metal fitted to a long handle that is used to remove goods from the oven
- **an oven scuffle and shaft**

- ○ two sets of **pastry cutters**, one fluted and one plain, which are used for cutting shapes out of pastry
- ○ one set of **piping tubes** and a **piping bag**, which are used for cake decoration. (By forcing icing through special piping tubes in a bag using skilful manipulation, artistic decorative effects can be achieved.)
- ○ one set of large **piping tubes** and **savoy piping bags**, which are used for depositing cake batter on baking trays or filling products with cream, etc.
- ○ various **pots** or **bowls** for holding ingredients
- ○ **rolling pins**
- ○ **balance scales and weights** (the number of sets of these weighing instruments will depend upon the size of the operation)
- ○ one set of **platform scales and weights**
- ○ **metal table scrapers**, which are used for scraping the sides of a mixing bowl
- ○ three **spatulas** – which are flat wooden implements used for stirring or beating small quantities of mixtures
- ○ **plastic storage baskets**, which should be large enough to hold 20 × 800g loaves
- ○ wheeled **metal bulk storage bins** for ingredients
- ○ **steel baking trays** (of varying sizes) on which bread and confectionery goods are baked
- ○ **strapped bread tins**, which are used for baking bread (800g – 3 or 4 per strap; 400g – 4, 5, or 6 per strap)
- ○ **lidded strapped bread tins**, which are used for baking bread (2 tins per strap for 2kg loaves for the hotel/restaurant trade)
- ○ **miscellaneous bread tins** for baking speciality bread
- ○ **small tart/cake tins**, which are small fluted and plain, patty pans and pie tins in which cake batter is baked. (Available in quantities sufficient to contain the batter of bulk recipes.)
- ○ **miscellaneous sizes** of **sandwich tins**, etc. for baking sponge-cake products
- ○ **cake hoops** and large cake tins of varying sizes in which cake batter is baked
- ○ four **sheathed dough-thermometers**
- ○ two **sugar thermometers** (if confectionery is part of output)
- ○ four to six **waste bins** for the safe and hygienic disposal of rubbish
- ○ **wheeled steel racks** for the temporary storage of products (e.g. bread resting in final proof or other products awaiting oven space)
- ○ **wheeled steel or wooden double-sized racks** (i.e. double length) with specially spaced shelving to accommodate cooling or cooled baked bread

Chapter 4
Raw Material Selection and Storage

To make good-quality goods, you need high-quality raw materials. Certain under- or over-sized fruits and vegetables (or those rejected because of surface blemishes) can be used if the variety is suitable but no food-processing operation should be carried out with anything other than the highest quality raw materials. It is not possible to improve the quality of a raw material by processing it. Poor-quality raw materials produce poor-quality preserved foods.

Handling

All raw materials should be handled with care to avoid bruising and damage. They should be transported in boxes or sacks and not thrown into piles in the backs of trucks. Foods should be kept off the ground and protected from insects which not only eat the food but also transfer spoilage and food-poisoning micro-organisms. Raw materials should be kept cool by storing them away from sunlight and they should be processed as quickly as possible before spoilage begins. Even a small amount of raw material that is spoiled by micro-organisms can quickly infect a whole batch.

Preparation

When fresh food is harvested, it is necessary to separate the good from the bad and to remove contaminants such as soil, leaves, insects and inedible parts. The cleaning and sorting of raw materials is a very cost-effective method for improving the overall quality of the food.

Cleaning

This removes the contaminants from food and makes it ready for further processing. Peeling fruits and vegetables, skinning meat or descaling fish are all types of cleaning procedures. Cleaning should take place as early as possible in the process to prevent time and effort being spent on food with contaminants that must then be thrown away. Removing rotting food at an early stage also prevents loss of the whole batch through the growth of moulds or bacteria during storage, or during delays in processing.

Foods can be cleaned by wet methods, for example, soaking and spraying, or by dry methods, for example, winnowing or sieving. Wet cleaning is more effective than dry methods for removing soil from root crops, or dust and pesticide residues from soft fruits or vegetables. However, wet procedures produce large amounts of dirty water that can cause pollution unless carefully disposed of. Clean water must be used to reduce the risk of contaminating the raw materials. Winnowing and sieving are used to clean dry foods such as grains, pulses and nuts that are hard enough to withstand the rougher treatment they receive by using this method. Care is needed to avoid excessive dust which recontaminates products and is a health hazard in itself.

Sorting

The sorting of foods is done by size, shape, weight or colour and should be carried out as early as possible to ensure a uniform product for later processing. Sorting by size (sieving) is particularly important when the food is to be heated or dried, as the rate of heating or drying depends in part on the size of the individual pieces. If there is too much variation, some pieces will be undercooked or still moist when others are properly processed. Weight sorting is more accurate than other methods but the additional cost of the equipment can only be justified for more valuable foods, for example, cut meats. Colour sorting is done by eye on a small scale as equipment that can do this is very expensive. Operators pick out discoloured food from a sorting table, or separate foods into different coloured batches for different products.

Weighing and measuring

The correct weighing out of raw materials and ingredients is critical to the success of a small business. It is worth investing in a suitable scale for weighing ingredients, ensuring that the operators responsible for formulating the batches are properly trained and ensuring that only high-quality ingredients are used. If scales are too expensive, simple scoops or measuring jugs should be used to ensure that the same amounts of ingredients are used for every batch.

Ingredients

Flour

Flour can be milled from a variety of cereals. The type of flour available in a region or country may depend upon the types of cereal grown.

Wheat flours

Wheat flour contains special storage proteins known as *gluten proteins*. Gluten proteins are capable of forming a strong, elastic network within the dough. This makes them particularly good for use when making leavened bread. As the yeast ferments, producing carbon dioxide gas, the protein network stretches and traps the gas. The gas trapped inside the dough gives the typical light texture of raised bread. If flours that are not capable of forming a strong, stretchy dough are used, the network snaps instead of expanding and the gas escapes. This results in a flat heavy bread.

The modern flour-miller can produce a range of flours for various uses in the baking industry. The main grades of wheat flour are determined by their extraction rates from the wheat grain to standards which are:

- o wholemeal flour – at 100 per cent extraction
- o wheatmeal flour – at 90–95 per cent extraction
- o straight-run flour – at 70–72 per cent extraction
- o patents – at 20–40 per cent extraction

The range of wheat flours available to bakers in different countries can be variations of these figures. The miller may also add traces of substances that serve to improve his products to suit the needs of the baker and the domestic customer. Wholemeal flour is used for the production of brown bread and rolls, and other high-fibre products.

Two by-products – wheat bran and pollard (which is used as a filler in the production of animal and poultry feeds) – can be manufactured from flour with a lower extraction rate. The wheatgerm that is extracted separately has a high nutritive value and is mainly used in the production of health foods and wheatgerm bread.

The following list details the various wheat flours available:

- o **Atta** is a flour of a quality suited to the production of chapattis, etc. It can also be produced in a wheatmeal quality.
- o **Special bakers' flour** (bread-making flour) is used for bread, rolls, and other fermented goods, and non-fermented products like pastry. Bakers' flour should possess characteristics in which the gluten is of good quality and strength and is fairly extensible. It must also stand up to the rigours of fermentation, even over lengthy periods, such as occurs in the sponge and dough process (described in Chapter 5). The gluten in this flour should also have sufficient elasticity in the fermenting dough to allow gas retention at the final proof to produce a loaf of good volume and with good oven spring when in the oven.

○ **Biscuit flour** is a special blend produced for mechanical biscuit plants.
○ **Self-raising flour** (SRF) is used for chemically aerated goods (such as soda bread). SRF is a soft flour fortified with a chemical aerating additive similar to baking powder. Many bakers prefer to make their own self raising flour in the bakery.
○ **Soft flour** is preferable for use in cake-making and other flour confectionery. However, in countries where the flour quality is variable, the baker should be prepared to make simple minor adjustments to the flour. For example:
  ○ when the flour available is too strong, the gluten-forming properties of the flour can be weakened by mixing in a proportion of weaker flour; mixing in a proportion of gluten-free ingredient to the flour (such as corn flour, rice flour or white, sifted fine maize-meal); or by taking care not to overmix the cake batter when incorporating the dry ingredients at the final stage.
  ○ when the flour available is too weak, it can be strengthened by mixing in a proportion of stronger flour; or after incorporating the dry ingredients at the final stage, the batter can be given a thorough beating for a couple of minutes which will slightly develop the weak gluten of the flour and strengthen the structure of the cake batter.

Non-wheat flours

There are a variety of non-wheat flours available, as listed below.

○ **Cassava flour** is a fine, white, powdery flour that has a shelf-life of up to one year under correct storage conditions. It is widely used as a staple food and for the small-scale production of a variety of fried and baked goods, including bread, and as a textile starcher and a source of starch in breweries. It has also been successfully used as a component of composite-flour biscuits. The best results are achieved by parboiling the cassava because the presence of modified starch is a significant help in water retention and not weakening the gluten. Cassava needs to be detoxified (through fermentation) to remove the components that yield cyanide. **Gari** is a creamy-white, granular flour that is produced from cassava tubers and can be eaten as a main meal with soup or stew.
○ **Cereal flours**, especially from **maize**, which is a staple in much of South America and Eastern and Southern Africa, and **sorghum**, a staple in semi-arid areas in Africa and India. They are also used

for the small-scale production of bakery products, snackfoods and as ingredients in other foods. The flours are fine and white (although incorporation of different quantities of bran alter the colour to pale brown). Under correct storage conditions the flours have a shelf-life of up to two years. A great variety of food products can be made from **maize** and it is the source of all corn flours that are used for baking powder fillings, custard and blancmange powders, etc. **Sorghum** is mainly used for the production of bread or porridge but can be further processed into a variety of foods such as snacks and beverages.

○ **Soy/composite flour** is a fine creamy flour that is combined with maize flour or other cereal flours to increase the protein content and balance the amino acid composition of the composite flours. In this form, it is used as a breakfast porridge and weaning food. The flour is hygroscopic (readily takes in and holds moisture) and should therefore be packaged in moisture-proof containers, e.g. strong polythene bags, and fully sealed.

○ **Shiro** (spiced flour from legumes) is a flour made of pre-cooked and spiced peas, broad beans or chickpeas. Its main use is to make a stew known as 'shiro wet'. Spices are mixed with the base material in appropriate proportions to give the taste associated with the product, and the mixture is then ground to a fine flour. Shiro can keep for over a year if it is stored in a dry place and packaged in plastic bags.

Yeast

Bakers' yeast is a living micro-organism (fungi) that causes dough to rise. When yeast is introduced to warmth, moisture and food it becomes active and starts to ferment. Yeast fermentation is the process by which sugars are converted to carbon dioxide, water, alcohol, energy and a range of secondary products, while at the same time the yeast reproduces itself.

Bakers' yeast can be obtained as compressed fresh yeast but is mainly available as dried yeast in tropical countries. Dried yeast is easy to transport and store and has a longer shelf-life than compressed yeast. It needs to be reconstituted in five times its own weight of warm water before it is used in a bakery. The amount of yeast added depends on the time and temperature of the fermentation process but is usually between 0.3 and 1.0 per cent of the flour weight.

Salt (sodium chloride)

Salt is obtained from two sources: rock salt and seawater. Owing to the possible presence of other salts and/or impurities in seawater, powdered rock salt is recommended for bakery purposes because it has a consistent quality, making it more suitable for fermented products. Salt should be clean, reasonably fine, free from large lumps and rapidly soluble.

Salt is used in the fermentation processes because:

○ it emphasizes flavour
○ it improves colouring
○ it reduces staling
○ it helps to strengthen the gluten of the dough
○ its inhibiting influence on yeast development acts as a restraining influence on the rate of fermentation.

Salt is hygroscopic and thus assists in helping to retain moisture in the baked loaf.

Salt should be added at around 2.5–3 per cent of the total weight of water (e.g. if the total weight of the water in the recipe is 50kg, the salt would be between 1.25 and 1.5kg). Care must be taken not to add too much salt as it can prevent the yeast from working properly. Salt should be stored in a dry position off the floor, with a clear space all round and well away from stored liquids, high humidity or damp.

Salt and yeast should not be allowed to come into direct contact with each other in the raw state because the salt will erode the yeast's cell walls and destroy the activity of the plasma inside the cell – resulting in poor or no fermentation.

Baking powder

Baking powder is a combination of two main ingredients, one alkaline (bicarbonate of soda) and the other acidic (cream of tartar or similar cream powder). When these ingredients are sifted and mixed together thoroughly and then moistened and heated, they will produce carbon dioxide (the aerating factor) and leave a residue in the product which should be harmless, colourless and free from any unpleasant taste or aroma. For the formula to be successful, the ratio needs to be two parts cream of tartar to one part bicarbonate of soda.

Sugar

Although flour should contain sufficient natural sugar, normally amounting to approximately 2.5–3 per cent, it will be found that a little sugar added to the yeast water will give a boost to the activation of the yeast. There are some countries where sweetened bread is popular, but, in general, only a modest addition is usual at an inclusion rate of between 1 and 1.5 per cent based on the total weight of flour in the recipe. The presence of a little added sugar will give a back-up to any deficiencies in local flour and will aid in the recovery of the dough from any slight felling action by the machines or other means.

Panela is unrefined sugar. It is a solid, black, crystalline sugar product made by concentrating sugar-cane juice. The sugar cane should be fresh and fully mature to obtain a good yield of juice. Panela has a shelf-life of more than a year and can be used instead of refined cane sugar as well as in traditional confectionery products.

Sugar of a fine, granulated quality is very suitable for cake-making and is normally readily available in most tropical countries. If properly balanced with the other ingredients, it has the power to lift and lighten the cake structure. It gives cakes their sweetness and provides a satisfactory crust colour. It also improves the eating and keeping quality.

Fats

Fats used in baking include butter, cake margarine, special bakers' fats and so on. In theory, the addition of fat is not necessary in a standard bread dough but the inclusion of fat (up to 1 per cent of the total flour weight) improves the loaf by giving an enhanced appearance, added softness and an improvement in the volume. The keeping quality and shelf-life of a loaf is better if fat has been added, and, depending upon its quality, the fat may lead to an improvement in the taste. A high-melting-point fat of vegetable origin is often preferred to a fat of animal origin. The use of edible oil instead of fat is not recommended.

Some bakers like to use up to 3 per cent fat. While this is unlikely to give additional enhancement to the general appearance of the loaf, it will increase the nutritional value. There may also be a slight improvement in the taste and keeping quality. Excessive use of fat is not to be recommended as it can adversely affect the fermentation and the volume of the loaf.

In cake-making, it is essential that the fat used has good creaming powers and that it is capable of holding the air being beaten into it. For best results, the fat should be fairly soft. Fat adds tenderness to the crumb, and during mixing prevents early toughening of the mixture. It increases the nutritional value of the food product and improves the flavour. Fat also has a beneficial effect on the volume of the finished product. The temperature of the fat and the other ingredients during the creaming process and the final incorporation of the flour should be approximately 21°C (70°F).

Eggs

Chicken's eggs are recommended as being very suitable for using in cake-making in tropical countries because of the availability of daily fresh supplies. Locally purchased eggs are rarely graded in size and so it is suggested that after shelling, the eggs should be weighed to obtain a standard quantity applicable to the recipe being used. The eggs should be fresh, with the whites and the yolks standing bold when cracked out of the shells.

Eggs form the strength and structure of the cake. They improve the flavour and, to a certain extent, improve the quality. If the amount of eggs being used in a recipe is increased, there should be a corresponding increase in the amount of fat – the quantity of eggs used in a recipe should be equal to or greater than fat. Similarly, if the amount of eggs is increased in a recipe containing milk, the quantity of milk should be reduced to offset the moistening properties of the additional eggs being used.

Milk

In certain types of cakes, fresh skimmed milk or reconstituted dried skimmed milk is very suitable for the baker to use. Sour milk or buttermilk is also useful in the bakery as the development of lactic acid contributes towards good volume in scones and buns. Reconstituted dried skimmed milk powder can be made up into a quantity of milk sufficient for the requirements of the recipe. In some instances, the milk powder can be mixed in directly with the dry ingredients, and then the water is added separately at a temperature suitable to the process involved.

Water

In many instances, particularly with fermented products, water comprises a substantial part of the total ingredients being used. In breadmaking, water is mixed with the flour to produce a strong, stretchy dough. The amount added depends on the type of flour but is usually half the weight of the flour used. The water should be slightly warm (body temperature is ideal), to encourage rapid fermentation by the yeast.

It is very important that the baker knows as much about the water being used as possible. It needs to be clean and *potable* (safely drinkable). Whether the bakery is a new business venture or has been recently acquired as a going concern, the water supply should be analysed, where possible, to confirm that there are no impurities present in it that could prove harmful to the product or to the consumer.

Water supplies and sanitation

As well as being a component of some foods, water is used for cleaning equipment and cooling containers. In all cases only potable water should be used and it may therefore be necessary to treat the water before it is used. There are two types of treatment: removal of suspended soils and removal/destruction of micro-organisms.

Suspended solids can be removed by allowing them to settle out in settling tanks and/or filtering the water through specially designed water filters. Both processes are relatively slow and large storage tanks are necessary if water is needed for washing or incorporation into the product. Some types of water filters remove micro-organisms but the easiest way of destroying them is to add a chlorine solution (5–8ppm final concentration of chlorine obtained by diluting bleach to 0.02–0.04 per cent). If the water is to be used in a product lower chlorine levels (e.g. 0.5ppm) are needed in a product in order to prevent an 'off' flavour. Chlorination of water supplies can be simply arranged by allowing bleach to drip, at a fixed rate, into storage tanks or pipelines. The rate of bleach addition is found by experiment, using simple chlorine paper or more sophisticated probes to check the chlorine concentration. A less suitable alternative is to boil water to sterilize it. Water should be heated to boiling and then boiled vigorously for at least ten minutes. This method has a high-fuel requirement and therefore increases processing costs.

Soft and hard water

Hard water has magnesium and calcium ions in solution which can make it difficult to make soap lather. Soft water is generally free from magnesium and calcium salts – either naturally or artificially. Both soft and hard waters can be used to make satisfactory doughs. Using hard water may result in an initial slowing down in the rate of fermentation at the start and a tendency to make 'tight' doughs. It may be necessary to increase the bulk fermentation time (see figure 5.2), or slightly increase the level of the yeast, or even slacken the doughs a bit. Knowing the exact characteristics of the water being used helps to make a decision about how to improve the product.

It is recommended that bakers using hard water ensure that the yeast is fully activated before adding the yeast water to the mixing dough. Where a stiffening in the dough beyond normal is experienced, consideration should be given to slackening the dough to normal viscosity, with the addition of a little extra water.

pH value of water

Water comes in a range from acid to alkaline and this is expressed in terms of hydrogen ion concentration. Neutral (non-acid or alkaline) water is classified as pH7. Any classification figure above 7 is becoming increasingly alkaline, and, any figure under 7 is becoming increasingly acidic. The length of time needed to mix the dough depends, in part, upon the pH of the dough. Alkaline doughs take longer to mix than acidic doughs. Fermenting dough has a pH value between 5 and 6.

Pre-mixes in the bakery

Manufactured pre-mixes are becoming more and more readily available to bakers in the form of improvers and anti-mould preparations, etc. Within the bakery, 'in house' improvers can be prepared on-site and provide greater ingredients control, time-saving during critical periods in the production flow and sufficient work for the production shift to be continuously and gainfully employed.

Pre-mixes contain all the dry ingredients of a recipe, including any milk powder, with any fat rubbed well into the mixture. Only the addition of water, and possibly some eggs, is then required before the mixture can be further processed into dough, cut into pieces, shaped, tinned and finished off ready for the oven. Mixing a pre-mix is a simple procedure of assembling all the ingredients (for example, salt, dough sugar and fat/margarine) in a mixing bowl and mixing together until they are all thoroughly incorporated.

Using a pre-mix reduces the number of ingredients that need to be weighed individually and so takes pressure off the mixing operators and saves time. It also reduces the risk of any ingredient being forgotten. Pre-mixes can be produced during a slack period in the shift and used for the next day's requirements or at a time when the throughput is in full swing. The same person should always carry out the weighing up and the mixing of the pre-mix.

Chapter 5
Making Bread

The processes described in this chapter are suggested as suitable for the initial stages of setting up a bakery. They should, of course, be adapted as necessary to suit local market preferences. However, the general principles and procedures remain the same so that it should be possible to use these standard processes as a basis for planning individual routines and procedures.

Basic baking skills

Kneading is a process of rolling and folding the dough so that all the ingredients are uniformly mixed and the dough becomes stretchy and pliable. Air is incorporated into the dough during kneading. The dough is removed from the mixing bowl onto a floured surface and kneaded by hand. The kneading stage is of vital importance because it allows the formation of the protein structure that will later trap the gas produced by the yeast, causing the bread to rise.

Proving The kneaded dough is covered with a damp cloth to prevent the dough surface drying out and hardening, and then it is placed in a warm place (about 26–30°C) to allow the yeast to ferment and the dough to rise. During this time the dough should double in size due to the air trapped inside it.

Knocking back After proving, the dough is kneaded again to release some of the carbon dioxide which has become trapped inside the dough and to improve its texture and elasticity.

Preparing the dough

There are a number of different processes in bread-making – some relatively simple to employ, others more sophisticated and requiring the use of special dough mixers and the inclusion of certain expensive additives which in many places are difficult to obtain.

Sponge and dough process

The sponge and dough process is suitable for small bakeries where there is no mechanical dough mixer available or other ancillary equipment for mechanical handling and the whole process can be completed by hand. The advantages of this process are better flavoured bread, better keeping quality and, often, better appearance.

The sponge and dough process can be broken down into two parts. First, a 'sponge' in the form of a slack to stiffish batter is set at a prescribed temperature in a dough trough using part of the flour, the yeast, a little sugar and part of the water all thoroughly mixed together. This is covered and left to sit for a length of time to ferment (the period of time being determined by the quantity of yeast used – it can be for as long as 14 or 16 hours). At the doughing stage, the remainder of the flour, sugar and water, the bakers' fat or margarine, the salt and, on occasions, a little booster of yeast according to the recipe, are added to the sponge and thoroughly mixed together to obtain a smooth, slightly slack to stiffish dough. The final dough-mixing by hand is strenuous for the dough maker but properly made bread using this process has an excellent flavour and enjoys an enhanced keeping quality. Figure 5.1 shows this process in the form of a flow diagram.

The lengthier fermentation times for the sponge are more suitable to the single-handed baker who can set the sponge in the afternoon (between, for example, 4pm and 6pm). The sponge can then be processed into dough from around 6am the following morning, thereby allowing the baker adequate time for rest. There is also a great saving in yeast usage by this process which can prove substantial in the costings.

We will now look in more detail at each of the stages shown in Figure 5.1.

Preparation
The ingredients for the sponge are weighed and/or measured, and the sponge-water temperature is calculated to ensure that the desired sponge temperature is obtained (see later). The quantity of yeast to be used is then determined, based upon the length of time the sponge will be left to set. The longer the setting time, the less yeast required.

Mixing
The sponge ingredients are then mixed to give a stiff batter. This can be done by hand or by mechanical mixing.

Process	Notes
Prepare ingredients ↓	Weigh/measure the raw ingredients, calculate the water temperature and quantity of yeast required.
Sponge mix ↓	Mix the sponge ingredients, by hand or mechanical mixer, to give a stiff batter.
Set ↓	Leave the batter in a covered bowl for at least five hours.
Dough mix ↓	Add the remaining ingredients to the batter and mix by hand or mechanical mixer to give a developed dough.
Divide ↓	Cut the dough into suitable sized pieces.
Ball mould ↓	Form the dough into balls by hand or with a mechanical moulder.
Interim rest ↓	Leave the dough balls to rest for up to 20 minutes.
Mould and tin ↓	Re-mould the rested dough balls by hand or with a mechanical moulder. Place the moulded dough into greased bread tins.
Final proof ↓	Place the tins in a steam proving-chamber or cover tins with a damp cloth and place in a warm, draught-free area for up to one hour.
Bake	Bake in a hot oven (204°C or 400°F) for 30 to 40 minutes.

Figure 5.1: A flow diagram showing the sponge and dough process

Setting

When the sponge is mixed, the temperature is read and recorded. The mixing bowl/dough trough is covered with a damp cloth and the sponge is allowed to ferment in a draught-free position.

Dough mix

The remaining ingredients for the bread are weighed and/or measured and added to the sponge. The sponge temperature is read and recorded and the temperature of the dough water required to obtain the desired dough temperature is calculated (see later in this chapter). The mixture is then mixed into dough. If mixing by hand, the total water content of the dough (including the amount of water used for the sponge) should be approximately 60 per cent of the total flour. If the mixing is by machine, the dough needs to be a little stiffer to prevent it sticking on the machines (i.e. on the make-up plant) and the water content should be about 57–59 per cent of the total flour.

The dough is mixed until all of the ingredients are uniformly combined and the dough becomes stretchy and pliable. Air is incorporated into the dough during the mixing. This stage is vital because it allows the formation of the protein structure that will later trap the gas produced by the yeast, causing the bread to rise.

Divide
The dough is then divided into suitable sized pieces according to its intended use (e.g. loaf or bread rolls). This is carried out either mechanically, or by cutting and scaling by hand.

Ball mould
The dough pieces are moulded into balls using either an umbrella moulder or by hand.

Interim rest-period
The balled pieces are either mechanically passed through and rested in a moving interim-prover, or they are set aside by hand in special drawers in order to rest before final moulding. The rest period varies according to the size of the dough piece but is approximately 12 minutes – or even, where necessary, up to 20 minutes.

Mould and tin
The dough is then moulded to the required size either mechanically by a final moulder or by hand. The moulded dough pieces are placed into straps of greased tins with the closing seams downwards and then the straps of three, four or five loaves are racked into a wheeled trolley.

Final proof
The racked trolley is wheeled into a steam proving-chamber (optimum humidity is approximately 85 per cent and the chamber temperature between 35°C and 43°C). If no steam proving-chamber is available, to prove the dough, the trolley is covered with damp cloth sheets and placed in a warm, draught-free, humid area. If a little steam can be introduced under the sheets so much the better (e.g. a large boiling kettle with a rubber-tube attachment that can be kept topped up and steaming).

Bake
When the dough pieces have doubled in size, they are baked in a pre-heated oven at 230–260°C. They may be brushed with milk to give a

shiny glaze to the top. The baking time depends on the size and type of bread, the number of loaves in the oven and the type of oven. With practice and familiarity, a baker knows accurately how long different types of bread take to bake. When properly baked the loaf should make a hollow sound when tapped on the base with the fingers. The loaves should be removed from the baking tins and placed on wire trays to cool.

The straight-dough process

With the exception of very small dough, the straight-dough process is really only suitable for mechanical mixing. In the production of straight dough, all the ingredients are mixed together at one time. Before mixing starts, the yeast is activated in a little of the dough water. The temperature of the main dough water is adjusted to produce a pre-determined dough temperature, which, together with the quantity of yeast employed determines the length of the bulk fermentation. It can be either 'no-time dough' which is processed into loaves virtually immediately after the dough has been mixed, or a dough that is mixed and allowed to sit fermenting in bulk (covered with a damp sheet) for a period of one hour's bulk-fermentation time (BFT) or as much as ten to twelve hours.

With the straight dough process, at about three quarters of the way through the estimated BFT period, the dough will have swollen to around its fullest extension and, at this stage, it is necessary to expel all the gas from the dough. This is known as the 'knock-back'. This can be done by hand, or by using a machine that artificially collapses the dough. The temperature is even throughout the dough, so the yeast starts to function again and generates more gas. With a sponge that has a much lower viscosity than a dough, no knock-back is required as the sponge collapses of its own accord and then rises up again. Like the sponge and dough process, the length of the period of bulk fermentation of the straight dough is controlled by the dough temperature and the quantity of yeast employed. The sequence of the production flow in this process is as shown in Figure 5.2. We will now go through each stage of the process in more detail.

Preparation

The ingredients for the bread are weighed and/or measured, and the dough-water temperature is calculated to ensure the desired dough temperature (see later in the chapter). The length of the BFT and the quantity of yeast required are then calculated. *The BFT includes the period from the finish of the mixing of the dough until the start of the cutting of the dough into pieces.*

Process	Notes
Preparation ↓	Weigh/measure the raw ingredients, calculate the water temperature and quantity of yeast required.
Mix ↓	Mix the ingredients together with a mechanical mixer.
Fermentation ↓	Leave the dough to ferment in a warm, moist area.
Knock-back ↓	The risen dough is kneaded to knock out the air.
Fermentation ↓	Return the dough to the fermenting area.
Knock-back ↓	The dough is briefly kneaded again to knock out the remaining air.
Divide ↓	Cut the dough into suitable sized pieces.
Ball mould ↓	Form the dough into balls by hand or with a mechanical moulder.
Intermediate proof ↓	Leave the dough balls to rest for up to 20 minutes.
Mould and tin ↓	Re-mould the rested dough balls by hand or with a mechanical moulder. Place the moulded dough into greased bread tins.
Final proof ↓	Place the tins in a steam proving-chamber or cover tins with a damp cloth and place in a warm, draught-free area for up to one hour.
Bake	Bake in a hot oven (204°C or 400°F) for 30 to 40 minutes.

Figure 5.2: A flow diagram of the straight dough process

Mixing

The flour and salt are mixed in a large bowl. The yeast is made into a smooth paste with a little sugar and warm potable water. The yeast paste, together with the remainder of the water, is added to the flour mix and thoroughly mixed to form a dough, in accordance with the recommendations accompanying the machine manual. *In the instance of large dough, this process is unsuitable for mixing by hand.*

The dough is mixed until all of the ingredients are uniformly mixed and the dough becomes stretchy and pliable. Air is incorporated into the dough during the mixing. As before, this stage is vital because it allows the formation of the protein structure that will later trap the gas produced by the yeast, causing the bread to rise.

Fermentation

The dough is left to ferment in a warm, moist environment for up to four hours. During this time, the dough will almost double in size due to the air trapped within it. If the bread is allowed to ferment for too long, too much air will be formed. This causes the dough to overstretch and so the air escapes and results in a hard, flat bread. A 'no-time' dough is given a short rest and then processed through the make-up plant into bread.

Knock-back

The knock-back is carried out after approximately three quarters of the bulk fermentation time, for example, on a four-hour BFT dough, the knock-back should be at the end of the third hour. This is when all the gas is expelled from the dough, which is normally achieved by a couple of minutes in the mixer. This levels the temperature throughout the dough and brings the yeast back into close contact with its food.

Second fermentation stage

The concluding part of the BFT, just before dividing and scaling starts, ensures that all the gases are expelled from the dough using a final short knock-back by hand. The remainder of the process is the same as for the sponge and dough process detailed above.

Ferment and dough

In the manufacture of certain types of rolls and fermented buns or cookies, the recipe often recommends this method. It involves a short period of fermentation – i.e. a thin sponge that rises quickly in around 20 to 40 minutes (depending upon the recipe) is then doughed up and produces very good-quality soft rolls, soft buns and cookies.

Other processes

Processes for cake-making, chemically aerated goods and various pies, tarts and patties are dealt with in Chapter 9 of this book.

Baking

Care should be taken not to over-prove products before putting them into the oven because over-proofing prevents oven spring, i.e. the expansion in size gained during baking. To avoid skinning, i.e. the hard crust which forms on dough when left uncovered, products should not be brought to the oven mouth and left sitting uncovered for any length of time. The production flow should be arranged to allow the oven space to be kept as full as possible. Any bottlenecks of fermented products waiting to be baked should be avoided.

Handling after baking

De-panning

After baking, the bread should be de-panned as soon as possible (i.e. tapped out of the tins). At this stage, care should be taken to avoid breakages or staining loaves on dirty de-panning tables or by using dirty oven gloves. Those people de-panning should have clean hands and/or use clean heat-protection gloves. The de-panning table and the bread-storage/-cooling racks must also be cleaned regularly to avoid staining the bread. To avoid breakages, and/or squashed loaves, care must be taken to ensure that the loaves are not thrown or heaped on top of each other.

Hot bread is quite fragile when withdrawn from the oven and should be allowed to sit in the tins for a few minutes in the racked trolley before being de-panned. However, it should not be allowed to sit and sweat in the tins. After cooling a little in the tins, it should be stacked onto cooling racks with a small space between each loaf and its immediate neighbour in order to allow the circulation of air and to hasten cooling. Loaves should not be stacked on top of each other.

To avoid tin distortion (bumps, dents and twisted tins), a special de-panning table with a rubber edge should be constructed locally (see Appendices). If the bread tins are regularly cleaned and properly greased at de-panning time, the loaves should spring free of the tins easily but care must still be taken to ensure that the hot bread is handled gently.

Cooling

Cooling should preferably be natural. Intensive fan-cooling is expensive and can cause excessive loss of moisture and weight. Hot or warm loaves should not be stacked close together on the cooling racks but be kept just a little apart from each other to prevent 'sweating' and the sides of the loaves becoming wet from condensation. Similarly, loaves should not be packed on top of each other until properly cooled, nor packed to a depth where the upper layers of loaves become heavy enough to squash the lower layers.

Slicing and wrapping

This is an expensive process unless the costs of doing this can be included in the selling price. The new baker should resist slicing and wrapping as unless it is done on a very large scale with automatic machines there is little profit benefit to the baker. Other inhibiting features include the problem of keeping the slicer blades continuously clean in order to avoid the transfer of bacteria from the blades (which can cause shelf-life problems). Bagged but unsliced bread may be a viable compromise.

Transport and distribution

On no account should warm bread be loaded into delivery vehicles. Delivery vehicles should never be overloaded. All delivery vehicles should have a load limitation, be properly shelved inside, and have 'check bars' provided to stop loaves falling from the shelves when the vehicle is in motion.

Baked bread should be passed on to the sales and despatch area where stocks should be regularly monitored to ensure that they are being sold in rotation and that any surplus unsold stocks are kept to a minimum.

Once a bakery has developed to the extent that a delivery service can be introduced (with delivery salespeople out developing their respective areas and touting for sales) there will be a need to train sales staff to a level at which they can advise customers on how to increase the sales of bakery products. The following salient points should be covered.

- o The retail outlet should be potentially suitable for the development of bakery sales.
- o The salesperson should seek to gain the shopkeeper's agreement that:
  - o all purchases of bakery goods will be on a cash basis
  - o a prime selling-spot within the shop will be available for the display and sale of bakery goods
  - o no strong-smelling products (e.g. soaps, soap powders, paraffin, etc.) will be stored or positioned close to bakery products
  - o no bakery goods can be accepted back by the bakery other than when there are genuine complaints. (NB: the shopkeeper's profit margins should be sufficient to allow him to accept this and act as a spur for him to sell more products.)
- o If the bakery agrees to any discount incentives, these must be very strictly linked to purchases made by the shopkeeper.

○ The bakery salesperson must give a first-class service within the above-mentioned guidelines at all times.

Calculating the sponge and dough temperatures

To achieve a good fermentation, the temperature of the sponge or dough should be maintained at between 32°C and 35°C (89°F to 95°F) as this represents the optimum range for the yeast's activity. Of the two main ingredients (flour and water), water is the one which can be most easily subjected to temperature change to a level that when it is mixed with the flour at a known temperature it will achieve the desired temperature. For accuracy, a thermometer is required to calculate water temperatures for fermented doughs. A metal-sheathed thermometer is preferable because an unsheathed thermometer may break and the broken glass may get into the ingredients or dough.

The straight-dough process – doubling method

Each recipe for fermented dough recommends a temperature figure for the 'mixed' dough – referred to as the 'dough temperature'. The formula for the doubling method is:

dough temperature × 2 − *flow temperature* = *the temperature at which the water should be taken.*

The straight-dough process – major factor method

This method requires accurate temperature readings to be recorded progressively on the dough sheets throughout total production every day. It also requires a record of the ambient (surrounding air) temperature of the dough-mixing room. The quality of the bread should be monitored throughout production, until the day when it is perfect for either one dough, or a few – or even throughout the day. At this point, the temperature readings of the dough that produced the perfect bread should be studied along with the recorded temperatures of the flour, water and air. Once the similarities have been recorded, the 'major factor' figure for the bakery will have been found. For future doughs, the major factor figure less the sum of the flour and bakery temperatures will give the temperature at which the dough water should be taken.

Sponge and dough system

Setting sponge in hot climates can be difficult, and suitable temperatures can vary between 21°C and 26°C (70°F and 80°F) depending upon the bakery site, and whether the night temperatures are hot and humid or inclined to be cool, or even chilly, when compared with temperatures during the day.

The following is the formula given by W.J. Fance in his book, *Students' Technology of Breadmaking and Flour Confectionery* published by Routledge and Kegan Paul, London, 1986.

$$\frac{(desired\ sponge\ temperature\ -\ flour\ temperature)\ \times\ weight\ of\ flour\ (in\ grams)}{weight\ of\ water\ (in\ grams)\ \times\ 2}$$

When mixing a sponge with flour, other ingredients and water into a dough, a simple formula to find the required water temperature is:

$$(desired\ dough\ temperature\ \times\ 3)\ -\ (flour\ temperature\ +\ sponge\ temperature)$$

Loss of weight during the fermentation process, baking and cooling

In calculating the yield of bread from dough, allowances should be made for a loss of dough weight attributable to the effect of the developing yeast in the dough's structure and the loss of gas during knock-back (about 1 per cent loss). The loss of moisture by evaporation during baking, de-panning and cooling can result in a further weight loss of between 9 and 11 per cent. Therefore, the dough piece should weigh 560g to obtain a 500g baked loaf and 880g to obtain an 800g loaf.

Correcting mistakes

Everyone can make mistakes. In baking, correcting them, or trying to determine the cause of the problem, can sometimes prove difficult.

The charts in Figures 5.3 and 5.4 list possible causes of faults in bread-making (both external and internal) and are designed to enable the beginner to detect the likely cause as well as to serve as a means towards correcting the situation.

Although certain faults (e.g. lack of volume) can be caused through a number of interrelated reasons, once some of the associated possible causes have been eliminated by the cross-reference procedure in these charts, it should be possible to detect the real reason for the problem.

Systems for small and medium sized bakeries

In order to be successful, any manufacturing business needs to operate systematically and this is particularly true of bakeries. Baking is not a complete science, and bakery production activity is subject to a varying set of circumstances (some seasonal and some not), which if not

Nature of fault Possible causes	Lack of volume	Excess volume	Lack of crust colour	Excess crust colour	Shell tops
Dough too tight, more especially with tinned bread	x				x
Dough chilled during fermentation	x				
Dough temp. too high			x		
Dough skinnned during proof			x		
Dough too slack		x			
Dough under-ripe	x			x	x
Dought over-ripe	x		x		
Too much yeast for system employed			x		
Insufficient yeast for system employed	x			x	
Insufficient proof	x				x
Slack moulding		x			
Oven temp. too high	x			x	x
Oven temp. too low		x	x		
Too much salt	x			x	
Insufficient salt		x	x		
Over use of chemical/mineral improver in bakery	x			x	
Excess water			x		
Flour with high maltose figure				x	
Flour with low maltose figure	x		x		x
Overbleached flour	x				
Flour too strong for system employed	x				
Too much proof		x			
Crust formed before maximum expansion					x

Figure 5.3: A list of causes of external bread faults

Nature of fault / Possible causes	Coarse texture	Poor crumb colour	Crumbly texture	Streaks, cores, seams, condensation marks	Holes in crumb	Dryness and rapid staling	Damp clammy, or close crumb
Dough too tight, especially with tinned bread		x	x		x	x	
Dough chilled during fermentation				x	x		
Dough temp. too high		x	x	x	x	x	
Dough too slack	x	x					
Dough not properly mixed	x	x	(over) x	(under) x	x		
Dough scraps from machines, etc.		x		x	x		
Dough felling							x
Dough under-ripe			x		x	x (cold dough)	x
Dough over-ripe		x	x			x	
Flour not sifted/improperly blended in bakery				x			
Flour with low maltose figure							x
Flour with high maltose figure		x		x			
Too strong flour with excessive yeast					x		
Flour too strong for system employed		x			x		
Too much dusting flour and/or dough skinned during fermentation				x	x		
Rope disease							(Damp) x
Too much yeast for system employed		x	x		x		

Figure 5.4: A list of causes of internal bread faults

Nature of fault Possible causes	Coarse texture	Poor crumb colour	Crumbly texture	Streaks, cores, seams, conden-sation marks	Holes in crumb	Dryness and rapid staling	Damp clammy, or close crumb
Insufficient yeast for system employed					x		
Too much salt			x		x		x
Insufficient salt		x	x			x	
Overuse of mineral/ chemical improver in the bakery			x	x		x	
Overuse of milk, fat etc.			x				x
Grease from dividers				x			
Excessive grease in moulders				x	x		
Insufficient proof					x		
Too much proof	x	x			x		
Slack moulding	x				x		
Incorrect moulding		x		x	x		
Incorrect bashing of cottage loaves					x		
Oven temp. too high	x				x		
Oven temp. too low	x	x	x		x	x	
Flash heat in oven					x		
Excessive top heat in oven					x		
Insufficiently baked							x
Incorrect cooling				x			

Figure 5.4 (cont.): A list of causes of internal bread faults

controlled can affect performance. Consequently, the baker must strive to maintain a regularity of temperature and humidity control in the processes and operate under ambient circumstances which can change from season to season and day to day – temperature and humidity can rise and fall during both day and night time.

The systems control imposed on a particular bakery is usually similar to others. It is in the ambient conditions where the differences are found, even at two bakeries sited close to each other. The baker must learn to adjust processes accordingly. The system merely requires the accurate recording of the actual facts concerning the storage of materials, the production flow, and the progression of sales and despatch. Consequently, the system must be in place for a little while before fine tuning adjustments can be made towards ensuring that the stores, the production, the sales and the despatch are all synchronised.

Chapter 6
Shelf-life of Bakery Products

The shelf-life of bread

The despatch area, where bread that is awaiting sale is normally stored, should be well ventilated, draught-free and ideally have an ambient temperature of between 21°C to 27°C (70 to 80°F). Bread should be treated differently according to how many days old it is.

First-day bread: Over the day, the bread condition will progress from oven fresh to fresh but at all times it will still be in excellent condition and pleasing to eat.

Second-day bread: The bread will still be soft and edible but when cut, the crumb will have developed a firmness not evident in first-day bread. At the end of the second day, this bread should be cleared at a reduced price, preferably well away from the bakery.

Third-day bread: This is still edible but there is a slight possibility of mould developing towards the end of the day. If this happens, the bread should be thrown away or burnt and the area where it was sitting should be thoroughly cleaned.

Moulds and rope development in bread

The speed of mould development in bread varies according to temperature and the degree of humidity of the storage conditions – which is slower at lower temperatures and which becomes more rapid as temperature rises. Mould contamination can be transferred by direct contact or by mould spores which can float along air currents and re-settle in areas suitable to their development.

It is very important that suspect bread is not allowed back into the despatch area and never back into the baking hall.

Rope (*Bacillus subtilis mesintericus*) is a bacteria of the soil that can transfer to growing wheat and eventually end up in a dormant state in the flour. Rope is heat-resistant and therefore is not killed off in the oven. However, its subsequent development under warm and humid conditions can be retarded by acidity and many bakers dose their dough with vinegar or acetic acid at 12.5 per cent strength, at a dosage of half to one litre per 90kg of flour used. Like moulds, rope will thrive in hot and humid conditions. It will first show as brown spots on the crumb which will evolve into sticky patches that can be pulled by the fingers into long spider's web like strands. It also gives off a smell which has been likened to rotting fruit and cat's urine. Rope is not toxic but the appearance of an infected loaf is such that no one would eat it.

The shelf-life of other baked products

Unless packaged, most cakes and biscuits have a shelf-life of only a few days. Biscuits need to be stored in a low-moisture environment or they will absorb moisture from the air and become soggy. If they contain a high proportion of fat, they must be stored away from light, air and heat to prevent the development of an off flavour due to rancidity.

Cakes need to be stored in a cool place away from heat to prevent them from drying out and becoming stale. Fruit cakes have a dense structure and so can be stored for much longer than light cakes. If the fruit cake is coated with marzipan (ground-almond paste) and icing, it can be stored in a cool, dark place for several months or even years.

Packaging

The packaging of baked goods can extend their shelf-life considerably. Biscuits should be packaged in material that prevents moisture being taken up from the atmosphere. The packaging used for light cakes and biscuits made with fat should be air-tight to prevent rancidity. Plastic films, glass jars or metal tins are all acceptable packaging materials. Bread is usually eaten within two days of purchase and so a simple paper or polythene wrapping is sufficient to protect it. If polythene is used, the bread must be cool before it is packed or water will condense inside the packaging, leaving wet spots that cause mould growth. All packaging material must be clean and dry before it is used in order to prevent contamination with spoilage or pathogenic micro-organisms.

Unsold bakery products

A bakery that ends up with a stock of unsold short shelf-life products at the end of any trading day (particularly if the stocks are sizeable) is likely to suffer a loss of profit, should these stocks remain unsold.

The possible causes of unsold stocks building up include:

o over-ordering
o over-production

o production throughput running late for distribution
o customers failing to accept orders from the delivery salesmen
o customers who normally collect failing to turn up
o unexpected competition in the field
o a driver salesperson failing to keep to his delivery times
o a credit customer falling behind in payment and suddenly reverting to cash with order
o a drop in quality
o drop in sales activity.

Careful checking should determine which one or more of the above factors has been responsible for your unsold goods, and help you plan to overcome the problem.

The following lists suggest various courses of action that can be taken to avoid this problem.

Possible action by the sales team

o Realistic forward-sales figures should be produced.
o A close co-operative liaison should exist between the person/ people responsible for sales and the customer (e.g. shop traders) regarding day-to-day requirements (including any stock build-up and order adjustments) and the passing on of advance knowledge back to the bakery as soon as possible.
o The sales team should establish good selling sites in key positions, which are likely to be able to take additional stocks later in the trading day, and likely to respond to a late-delivery incentive discount.
o The sales team should have a close liaison with hoteliers, hostels, institutions, and catering establishments who can handle day-old bread without greatly affecting their quality standards.

Possible action by the production team

o The production department should try to develop a few products in which it is possible to use fresh breadcrumbs (or fresh cake-, bun- and scone-crumbs) as one of the main ingredients. For example, meat lines using breadcrumbs as part of the filler.
o In certain breads, fresh white breadcrumbs can be recycled as a part of the recipe.
o Dried white breadcrumbs can be supplied to hoteliers, and caterers as fish dressing.
o If it is possible to create a small simple bakery unit away from the general production area, it may be a viable proposition to produce poultry crumbs and poultry mash, taking advice from

the manufacturers of vitamin concentrates, and using bakery stales as the filler or a substantial part of the filler.

o As a last resort, although not profitably attractive, it is possible to dispose of stale produce along with bakery sweepings to a pig farmer.

Chapter 7
Hygiene and Safety

The production of safe food

Food is one of the few commodities that people actually ingest and so when it is being produced for sale there is a special responsibility not to hurt or injure customers. The main ways in which a producer can harm consumers are by selling food that contains:

○ poisonous materials
○ bacteria or moulds or the poisons they produce
○ glass or other contaminants that could cause harm if eaten.

Safe food can only be produced by *careful attention to hygiene* and by *good quality-control* during production, storage and distribution.

Good hygiene means careful attention to the cleanliness of:

○ the building
○ the processing equipment and
○ the personal hygiene of food-handlers.

This will prevent the bacteria that are present in the building, or on equipment and food-handlers, from growing in the food.

Good quality-control means ensuring the:

○ selection of good-quality raw materials and the correct recipe
○ maintenance of correct processing conditions in relation to temperature and times of heating
○ prevention of contaminating materials such as dirt, metal and stones from becoming mixed with the food
○ use of packaging materials to protect the food after processing
○ control of storage conditions to stop the food becoming infected after processing.

These factors will ensure that only wholesome food without contaminants is produced. Any bacteria in the raw materials will be destroyed or controlled at a safe level and prevented from growing during storage.

Although food laws may be enforced by public health inspectors or people with similar jobs, it is the customer who will judge and inspect on a regular basis the foods made by producers. If customers become ill from eating a food or think they are being cheated or mis-led, they won't buy the food again. It is therefore in the producers' own interest to make safe, wholesome foods so that customers buy again and the business grows and succeeds. In the end, the customer is the most effective food inspector.

Good hygiene

The following are all essential tips for ensuring good hygiene.

- All utensils must be washed daily or once they have been discarded in a soiled state.
- All baking trays and baking tins must be cleaned daily and given subsequent regreasing with edible oil/fat as required.
- All baking tables and machines must be washed daily as directed. Certain machines require partial dismantling by the person in charge of them so they can be cleaned, and the cleaner should assist only if requested.
- There should be a daily routine of sweeping, wiping, and wet-mopping the walls, oven exteriors and other fixed fittings. (Care must be taken around electric switches and fittings, with regard to wet mopping, to avoid any possibility of electric shock.)
- Dry sweeping should also take place, with inaccessible places being cleaned by either a vacuum or a blower arrangement.
- There should be regular emptying of waste bins placed around the baking hall, as frequently as required. Waste can be further divided into:
  - returnable bags and containers that can go straight back to the main stores for return to the supplier
  - clean paper and cardboard which can be stored and sold to the scrap paper merchants if applicable
  - pig-food waste that can perhaps be sold.
- There should be weekly and occasional cleaning, such as the washing and scrubbing of bakery racks and trolleys, wooden bakery trays, bread tins, etc. At a time suitable in the bakery routine, batches of items can be washed and dried.
- If there is a delivery vehicle, this must be swept out and/or wet-mopped each day.

Operator hygiene

The foods that carry the greatest risk of infection from operators are those that are handled after they are cooked (e.g. fried snack foods, cooked meats) and those that are not heated before sale (e.g. sausages and other meat products, ice cream and other dairy products). However, infection can be minimized by adopting the following rules in all food-processing premises.

- ○ Educate workers in the dangers of poor hygiene using books, films, or videos, etc. Regular guidance and training should be given to all food handlers, so that hygiene is seen as important. Relevant posters should be displayed in the locker room and toilet/shower areas.
- ○ Do not allow people to work if they have a cough, serious cold or influenza, boils or other skin infections or stomach complaints (e.g. sickness or diarrhoea). It is not sufficient to cover skin complaints with a bandage or gloves. If necessary, insist on a medical examination of suspect workers.
- ○ All employees should scrub their hands thoroughly (for more than 30 seconds) using non-perfumed soap and clean water before starting work. Particular attention should be paid to ensuring clean nails. Towels should be provided and washed regularly. Hands should always be washed after using a WC.
- ○ All tools and work surfaces should be thoroughly and regularly washed with chlorinated water throughout the day.
- ○ Smoking should not be allowed because bacteria from the mouth can be transferred via the cigarette to the hands and hence to the food. Spitting should be prohibited for similar reasons.
- ○ All clothing should be clean. If necessary, aprons or coats should be provided and regularly washed. All food handlers must be extra careful with their personal hygiene, their uniforms, and any cuts or other sores on their hands and other parts of their bodies. Key production staff should wear rubber gloves. The shift manager must be extra vigilant in ensuring that waterproof dressings are used on cuts or sores and that these are replaced immediately if there is any sign of the dressing slipping off.

Control of moulds and pests

As you might expect of premises that contain perishable ingredients, bakeries can be particularly susceptible to infestation by pests, such as insects or rodents, and moulds. However, straightforward precautions can be taken, including the training of all staff to look out for and report immediately any evidence of possible infestation, pests or moulds within the bakery premises or vehicles.

Reduction of mould spores

There must always be efforts made towards reducing the number of mould spores floating around and to contain them at a level where their development is prevented or minimized. The cleaners should gather up all extraneous flour-dust by blowing and vacuuming the inaccessible areas under the machines and the work tables. They should ensure that there are no humid damp areas where bacteria can breed.

Anti-mould additives can be added to the recipes during the hot season. Baking-hall furniture and vehicle interiors can be sponged down by cleaning staff using a weak solution of vinegar and water. Care must be taken to prevent stale goods from getting back into the sales and despatch area, and in particular, the baking hall.

Stores

Stores must be kept clean, tidy and organized on a daily basis. When bulk stores arrive, someone should be in charge of making sure that new flour bags do not become mixed with older ones and that they are stored appropriately off the ground. All other ingredients should be stored together and with an emphasis on keeping them damp- and pest-free. Regular checks should be made.

General precautions

There should always be an adequate and continuous supply of clean water laid on, a good flow of cold water, and an adequate supply of hot. Any forward storage water tanks should be covered with a close-fitting lidded arrangement and should be regularly inspected for any evidence of contamination build-up (from flour dust, etc.).

Most contamination in a bakery usually emanates from carelessness or laziness in some shape or form, or from lack of proper supervision and control – for example, an accumulation of rodent droppings or an insect infestation being allowed to develop. Things to watch for are:

- infestations in storage rooms and floors
- contamination on the bread-slicer blades
- dried and damp dough-droppings
- cracks in working surfaces
- dirt build-up in window frames, under the machines and tables and in the toilet rooms area.

A few brightly painted waste-disposal bins should be placed around the bakery and be emptied regularly during the working day.

○ All toilets and wash basins should be provided with nail brushes for hygiene purposes.
○ Where possible, the bakery walls should be tiled up to a certain height.
○ Broken surfaces on walls and floors should be repaired right away.
○ The water runaway channels on the floor should be kept clear at all times and the drainage outlet points should be insect-proofed with fine mesh that can be removed, cleaned and replaced again right away.

Items that should be banned in the bakery

All bakery staff must be aware that certain items are not permitted within the working areas of the bakery for safety reasons.

○ No tumblers, bottles, china cups or similar glassware should be allowed into the bakery working area.
○ No strong-smelling soaps, detergents or disinfectants should be used in the bakery.
○ No indelible pencils should be used in the bakery.
○ All waste matter should be placed in dump bins and cleared regularly during the day. They should be taken to a refuse point well away from the bakery.
○ Personal clothing should be kept in the locker room, not in the bakery.

Operator Safety

Someone who is adequately trained in fire-fighting and in first aid should be available on each shift. Suitable fire-fighting equipment and a proper first-aid box should be ready to hand and regularly checked to make sure that they are complete and operational.

Fires

○ Do not attempt to fight a fire unless it is safe and you have called the emergency services.
○ Remove the casualty from danger, if it is safe to do so.
○ Do not enter a burning building.
○ Do not enter a smoke- or fume-filled room.

Treatment for burns

1. Cool burn
   - Make the casualty comfortable.
   - Pour cold liquid on injury for 10 minutes – do not use running water.

2. Remove any constrictions
   - Carefully remove any clothing or jewellery from the affected area before the injury starts to swell.

3. Cover burn
   - Cover the burn and surrounding area with a sterile dressing or a clean piece of material such as a tea towel (placed loosely over the burn), cling film or plastic bags full of water depending on the depth/degree of the burn.

4. Take or send casualty to hospital
   - Call an ambulance if you cannot transport the casualty to hospital.
   - Record details of the casualty's injuries and any possible hazards.

Precautions
   - Do not apply lotions, ointment or fat to a burn, or touch the injured area or burst any blisters.
   - Do not remove anything sticking to the burn.
   - If the burn is to the face, do not cover it. Keep cooling with water until help arrives.
   - If the burn is large or deep, treat the casualty for shock. Monitor and record breathing, pulse and level of response every 10 minutes.
   - If the burn is chemical, rinse for at least 20 minutes.

Clothing on fire

   - Either stop, drop, wrap or roll the casualty on the ground.
   - Or lay the casualty down, burning side upwards and douse him with water.
   - Do not use flammable materials to try to smother flames.
   - Do not let the casualty run about or go outdoors.

Electrical injuries

   - Stay clear of the casualty until the domestic current has been switched off.
   - Do not go within 18 metres of live high voltage electrical sources.

Severe bleeding

1. Apply pressure to wound
   - Remove or cut the casualty's clothing to expose wound.
   - If a sterile dressing or pad is immediately available, cover the wound.
   - Apply direct pressure over the wound with your fingers or palm of your hand.

2. Raise and support injured part
   - Make sure the injured part is above the level of the casualty's heart.
   - Lay the casualty down.
   - Handle the injured part gently if you suspect the injury involves a fracture.

3. Bandage wound
   - Apply a sterile dressing over any original pad and bandage firmly in place.
   - Bandage another pad on top if blood seeps through.
   - Check the circulation beyond the bandage at intervals; loosen it if needed.

4. Call ambulance if necessary
   - Give details of the site of injury and extent of bleeding.

5. Treat for shock and monitor casualty

Precautions
   - If there is an embedded object in the wound, apply pressure on either side of the wound and pad around it before bandaging.
   - If possible wear gloves to protect against infection.
   - If the casualty becomes unconscious, place in the recovery position and be ready to resuscitate if needed.

Eye injury

1. Support casualty's head
   - Lay casualty on back, holding the head on your knees to keep it as still as possible.
   - Tell the casualty to keep the 'good' eye still as movement of the uninjured eye may damage the injured eye further.

2. Give eye dressing to casualty
   - The casualty should hold a sterile dressing or clean pad over the injured eye, keeping the uninjured eye closed.

3. Take or send casualty to hospital
   - If possible transport the casualty lying down.

Precautions
   - Do not touch the eye or any contact lens, or allow the casualty to rub the eye.
   - If it will take some time to obtain medical aid, bandage an eye pad in place over the injured eye.

Shock

1. Lay casualty down
   - Use a blanket to protect him from the cold ground.
   - Raise and support the casualty's legs as high as possible.
   - Treat any cause of shock such as bleeding.

2. Loosen tight clothing
   - Undo anything that constricts neck, chest and waist.

3. Call ambulance
   - If possible call amulance, giving details of the cause of shock, if known.

4. Monitor breathing and pulse
   - Monitor and record breathing, pulse and level of response every 10 minutes.
   - Be prepared to resuscitate if necessary.

Precautions
   - Do not leave the casualty alone, except to call an ambulance.
   - Do not let the casualty eat, move, smoke or drink.

Chapter 8
Production of Different Breads

Process control

As mentioned in Chapter 4, to make good-quality goods you need high-quality raw materials. Flour must be free from foreign matter, soils and other contaminants, such as weevils. Good-quality, active yeast must be used in order to ferment the dough to the desired level within the required time. Flour, water and yeast should be in the right proportions to produce a fermented product of the required texture. Accurate weighing of all the ingredients is an important control point because small variations can cause significant differences in the final product. Thorough mixing and kneading of the dough will result in a uniform product.

Temperature and time control of the baking process are important to ensure the colour, texture and flavour qualities of the product.

Hygiene

As discussed in Chapter 7, hygienic practices are essential with respect to food handlers, raw materials, equipment and premises. Use potable water to avoid contamination. Containers used to ferment the dough and the storage baskets must be well cleaned before each batch.

Packaging and storage

Good packaging and storage control are necessary to prevent mould growth (see Chapter 6). The product should be properly cooled before packing because surface moisture encourages contamination. Polythene bags and paper bags provide protection against some insects and soil contamination. The product should be stored in a ventilated, cool, dry place, raised off the floor.

Recipes for various types of bread

We will now look at some recipes that can be useful for small-scale production. All quantities given in the ingredients are for the production of a commercial batch.

Brown wholemeal bread (no-time dough)

Ingredients
16kg bakers' strong flour
16kg wholemeal flour
485g ordinary dried yeast – the weight of ordinary dried yeast is calculated at 50 per cent that of fresh yeast, therefore double the quantities to arrive at the amount of fresh yeast required.
576g fine salt
370g granulated sugar
795g bakers' fat/margarine
19.2kg water

Equipment
Dough mixer
Bread-forming tables and moulds
Baking trays and ovens
Scales
Heat sealer (if polythene bags are used)

Process	Notes
Sift and mix	Sift the flour, mix in the wholemeal and rub in the fat.
	Disperse the yeast and a little sugar into a portion of water at a temperature of approximately 95°F (35°C) (approximately 5 to 10 times the yeast's weight in water). Stir vigorously. Leave for 12 minutes to allow yeast to activate.
	Add salt and remaining sugar into dough water and add to flour mixture.
	Once the dough water is almost drawn in, add the activated yeast and continue mixing until an elasticated dough is formed.
Rest	Cover the dough with a damp cloth for 20 minutes to rest.
Roll form	Divide the dough into equally weighed pieces and mould them.
	Put into interim prover for rest period and then through the mechanical moulder into a greased tin.

Final proof	Loaves are covered by damp cloths and put into a steam space or cabinet for final proofing.
Bake	Bake at 430°F (220°C) for 30 minutes for 500g loaf or 40–50 minutes for 800g or 1kg loaf.
Cooling	Remove the bread from the oven, de-pan, set apart on cooling racks and allow to cool.
Pack	Pack in paper or polythene bags depending on length of storage time before sale or consumption.

Standard white bread

Ingredients
90kg bakers' strong flour
910g ordinary dried yeast – the weight of ordinary dried yeast is calculated at 50 per cent that of fresh yeast, therefore double the quantities to arrive at the amount of fresh yeast required.
1.59kg fine salt
850g granulated sugar
910g bakers' fat/margarine
53kg water

Equipment
Dough mixer
Bread forming tables and moulds
Baking trays and ovens
Scales
Heat sealer (if polythene bags are used)

Process	Notes
Sift and mix	Sift the flour and mix in the fat.
	Disperse the yeast and a little sugar into a portion of water at a temperature of approximately 95°F (35°C) (approximately 5–10 times the yeast's weight in water). Stir vigorously. Leave for 12 minutes to allow yeast to activate.
	Add salt and remaining sugar into dough water and add to flour mixture.

Once the dough water is almost drawn in, add the activated yeast and continue mixing until an elasticated dough is formed.

Rest

The dough should rest in 'bulk fermentation' for about 45 minutes covered by a damp cloth.

Knock-back

After resting, the dough is knocked-back, i.e. all the gas is expelled from the dough and it is kneaded slightly (1 minute of mixing with a machine will achieve this).

Roll form

After a further 15 minutes (making the total bulk fermentation time (BFT) 1 hour), divide the dough into equally weighed pieces and mould into balls.

Cover with a damp cloth and rest for 10 minutes before final moulding.

Loaves being processed mechanically go through the umbrella mould, rest in the interim prover and are then put through the mechanical moulder into a greased tin.

Final proof

Loaves are covered by damp cloths and put into a steam space or cabinet for final proofing.

Bake

Bake at 430°F (220°C) for 25–30 minutes for 500g loaf or 40 minutes for 800g or 1kg loaf.

Cooling

Remove the bread from the oven, de-pan, set apart on cooling racks and allow to cool.

Pack

Pack in paper or polythene bags depending on length of storage time before sale or consumption.

White bread – overnight dough (12 to 14 hours)

Ingredients

Sponge	*Dough*
54kg bakers' strong flour	81kg bakers' strong flour
150g ordinary dried yeast	50g ordinary dried yeast (booster)
– weight of ordinary dried yeast	– weight of ordinary dried yeast

is calculated at 50 per cent that of fresh yeast, therefore double the quantities to arrive at the amount of fresh yeast required.
41kg water

is calculated at 50 per cent that of fresh yeast, therefore double the quantities to arrive at the amount of fresh yeast required.
2.445kg fine salt
1.99kg granulated sugar
1.35kg bakers' fat/margarine
40kg water

Equipment
Dough mixer
Bread forming tables and moulds
Baking trays and ovens
Scales
Heat sealer (if polythene bags are used)

Process	Notes
Sponge	
Sift and mix	Sift the flour.
	Disperse the yeast into 5–10 times its weight in water at a temperature of approximately 95°F (35°C) and set aside to activate for 12 minutes.
	Bring the sponge water to a temperature of 70°F (21°C) and mix into the flour.
	Immediately, add the activated yeast and water and mix together to obtain a soft batter type sponge.
	Record the sponge temperature on the production record.
Fermentation	Cover the sponge with a damp cloth and set in a draught-free place for 12–14 hours.
Dough	
Sift and mix	Sift the flour for the dough onto the sponge and rub in the fat.
	Disperse booster yeast into 5–10 times its weight in water at a temperature of 95°F (35°C). Add a little sugar. Whisk together and set aside to activate the yeast for about 12 minutes.

Disperse the salt and remainder of the sugar into the dough water (at a temperature of 80°F (26.7°C) and add to the other ingredients.

Start the mixer and as the ingredients are becoming absorbed add the booster-activated yeast water and continue mixing to obtain a stiffish dough which comes cleanly away from the side of the bowl.

Rest

The dough should rest for about 30 minutes covered by a damp cloth.

Knock-back

After resting, the dough is knocked-back, i.e. all the gas is expelled from the dough and it is kneaded slightly (1 minute of mixing with a machine will achieve this).

Roll form

Divide the dough into equally weighed pieces and mould into balls.

Cover with a damp cloth and rest for 10 minutes before final moulding.

Loaves being processed mechanically go through the umbrella mould, rest in the interim prover and are then put through the mechanical moulder into a greased tin.

Final proof

Loaves are covered by damp cloths and put into a steam space or cabinet for final proofing.

Bake

Bake at 430°F (220°C) for 25–30 minutes for 500g loaf or 40 minutes for 800g or 1kg loaf.

Cooling

Remove the bread from the oven, de-pan, set apart on cooling racks and allow to cool.

Pack

Pack in paper or polythene bags depending on length of storage time before sale or consumption.

Cheese loaf

Ingredients (for 8 or 9 loaves)
2kg soft flour
62g baking powder
31g fine salt
31g dry mustard
480g bakers' fat/margarine
1kg grated cheddar cheese
1.24kg milk

Equipment
Dough mixer
Bread forming tables and moulds
Baking trays and ovens
Scales
Cheese grater
Heat sealer (if polythene bags are used)

Process	Notes
Sift and mix	Sift and mix the flour, baking powder, salt and mustard together and then rub the fat into the dry ingredients.
	Mix in the grated cheese.
	Add the milk and mix in to form a soft smooth dough.
Roll form	Divide the dough into 539g pieces and mould into balls using minimum amount of dusting flour.
	Cover with a damp cloth and rest for 10 minutes before final moulding.
	Roll into sausage shapes of an even thickness, place neatly into a greased tin, pressing the loaf down level.
	Cover with a damp cloth and rest for a further 10 minutes.
Bake	Bake at approximately 400°F (204°C) for about 30 minutes, by which time the loaf should be firm to touch. After the bread has been in the oven for 20 minutes, lightly sprinkle some grated cheese over the top of each loaf.

Fermented sweet bread

This type of bread resembles a leavened biscuit with a soft texture and dark-brown toasted crust.

Ingredients
45.5kg soft wheat flour
11 litres water
11.35kg sugar
8.4kg lard (pork fat or hydrogenated vegetable oil)
1.35kg dried yeast
1.35kg baking powder
454g common salt
9kg eggs

Equipment
Dough mixer
Bread-forming table and moulds
Baking trays and oven
Heat sealer (if polythene bags are used)
Scales

Process	Notes
Raw material	Soft wheat flour, sugar, fat, water, yeast, eggs, baking powder, salt.
Mix	Mix together the flour and water.
	Mix in the sugar, fat, yeast, baking powder, salt and eggs to form the dough.
Rest	After thorough mixing, the dough is covered with a damp cloth or oiled polythene and left to rest for 20 minutes.
Roll form	Divide the dough into equally sized pieces, depending on final product size desired. Form each piece to a round shape and place on a tray.
Fermentation	Cover dough pieces with a damp cloth to prevent drying out. (The dough pieces may be coated with a layer of fat and sprinkled with flour.) Leave for 3 hours at a temperature of 20–24°C/68–72°F.

Bake	Bake at 180°C/350°F for about 25 minutes. For very large loaves, lower the temperature and bake for longer. The surface should be a dark-brown colour when baking is complete.
Cool	Remove from oven and cool sufficiently before packaging.
Pack	Pack in paper or polythene bags depending on length of storage time before sale or consumption.

Soda bread

Typical soda bread is round in shape and usually produced with a cross so it can be broken into four quarters. It is more raised in the top of the centre. It is brown in colour and has a yellow tinge throughout due to the soda. The texture is coarse and the product is firm to the touch.

Ingredients (8 loaves)
2.28kg soft flour
57g fine salt
80g bicarbonate of soda
1.6kg buttermilk
NB: if no buttermilk is available, replace the bicarbonate of soda with baking powder

Equipment
Dough mixer
Cutters/dough divider
Baking trays and oven
Scales

Process	Notes
Sift and Mix	Sift and mix the flour with the bicarbonate of soda.
	Disperse the salt into the buttermilk. Mix all the ingredients together to obtain a soft dough.

Roll form	Cut the dough into 500g pieces. Mould into ball shape and then into a sausage shape of even thickness, the length of the inside of the baking tin. Place each loaf into the greased baking tins and press level.
Rest	Cover with a damp cloth and rest for 5 minutes before putting it into the oven.
Bake	Bake at 215°C/420°F for 20–25 minutes.
Cool	Remove from oven and cool sufficiently before packaging.
Pack	Pack in paper or polythene bags depending on length of storage time before sale or consumption.

Fermented rolls (no-time dough)

Ingredients (770 rolls)
32kg bakers' strong flour
485g ordinary dried yeast – the weight of ordinary dried yeast is calculated at 50 per cent that of fresh yeast, therefore double the quantities to arrive at the amount of fresh yeast required.
580g fine salt
415g granulated sugar
640g skimmed milk powder
640g bakers' fat/margarine
19.2kg water

Equipment
Dough mixer
Baking trays and ovens
Scales
Heat sealer (if polythene bags are used)

Process	**Notes**
Sift and mix	Sift the flour and milk powder and mix in the fat.
	Disperse the yeast and a little sugar into a portion of water at a temperature of approximately 95°F (35°C) (approximately 5–10 times the

yeast's weight in water). Stir vigorously. Leave for 12 minutes to allow yeast to activate.

Disperse the salt and remaining sugar into the dough water and add to flour mixture.

Once the dough water is almost drawn in, add the activated yeast and continue mixing until an elasticated dough is formed.

Rest	Cover with a damp cloth and rest for 10 minutes.
Roll form	Divide the dough into 70g pieces and mould into balls.
	Cover with a damp cloth and rest for a few minutes.
	Using a rolling pin, roll the balls out into flattish rounds, approximately 8cm in diameter. Place onto lightly greased baking tray about 3cm apart.
Final proof	Cover the rolls with damp cloths and put into a steam space or cabinet for final proofing.
Bake	Bake at 460/480°F (237/250°C) for 15–18 minutes to obtain lightly baked, medium-baked or well-baked quality as desired.
Cooling	Remove the bread from the oven, de-pan, set apart on cooling racks and allow to cool.
Pack	Pack in paper or polythene bags depending on length of storage time before sale or consumption.

Difo Dabbo (whole-wheat fermented bread)

Difo Dabbo is a fermented and spiced whole-wheat flour bread. It measures about 60cm in diameter and is 5 to 7cm thick. The bread feels firm to the touch and sounds hollow if it is lightly tapped. It contains about 60 per cent moisture and is harder and cooked more on the bottom. It looks reddish brown depending on the colour of the seed used. It is very prestigious bread made during national holidays, marriage ceremonies, birthdays and religious festivals.

Equipment
Fermenting container
Bread pan (*metad*)
Straw basket
Stone mill

Process	Notes
Raw materials	Locally available wheat-grain with large and shiny seeds, i.e. hard wheat, is preferred.
Cleaning	Foreign materials are hand-picked and lighter impurities are winnowed to clean the seed.
Dehulling	The wheat grain is usually dampened and pounded with a traditional wooden mortar and pestle to remove the bran.
Grinding	Clean wheat is ground through a stone mill.
Dough making	One part flour, one half part warm water and about 1.4 per cent of dry yeast by weight of flour are mixed together, covered and left overnight to ferment.
	Add 5 times amount of original flour used and 3 times amount of warm water.
	Add black cummin and bishop weed seeds equal to 1 per cent each and 3 per cent of salt of the original weight of flour.
	Knead for 5 minutes, cover with a damp cloth and let stand for 2 hours.
Baking	The bread pan, known as a *metad*, is a flat, round clay griddle placed on triangular stands and covered with false banana or other large edible leaves.
	The dough is poured onto the leaves and patted down with wet hands into a uniform shape. It is then covered with false banana leaves. The lid is placed on the bread pan and covered with dry

pieces of broken cow-dung. Several pieces should be inserted underneath the *metad* to start a fire and then burning pieces should be transferred to ignite the cow-dung on the top.

The fire should be kept burning for 30 minutes to allow the bread to cook. Remove the bread from the *metad* and peel off the false banana leaves.

Electrical *metads* are available locally specifically for this purpose.

Process control
Flour, wheat, starter and spices must be in the right ratio to produce the desired texture and flavour.

The total fermentation period must not be longer than 16 hours before baking is started.

The bread must be cooked on both surfaces at the same time for no less than 30 minutes.

Hygiene
The fermenting container and storage baskets must be cleaned before starting to make *Difo Dabbo*. If a cow-dung fire is used, care should obviously be taken not to contaminate the product, or the ingredients.

Packaging and storage
Difo Dabbo stored in cool areas in straw baskets can last for 2 days with the minimum loss of water.

Ambasha (traditional fermented wheat bread)

Ambasha is a traditional fermented bread made from wheat flour. It is flat and round, measuring about 35cm in diameter and 2cm thick. Freshly made *Ambasha* is moderately soft containing about 65 per cent moisture. The front side is lightly brown and decorated with several lines while the bottom is darker with a smooth surface. *Ambasha* has a plain taste and is usually served during breakfast with tea. It is also widely eaten in factories, institutions and snack bars throughout the Arabic world.

Equipment
Traditional sieve
Fermenting container
Metad
Straw baskets
Polythene sheet
Stone mill
Plastic sealer

Process	Notes
Raw material	Wheat is the only raw material used for making *Ambasha*.
Cleaning	Foreign materials are hand-picked and lighter impurities are winnowed to clean the grain.
Dehulling	The wheat grain is usually dampened and pounded in a traditional wooden mortar and pestle to remove the bran.
Grinding	Clean, dehulled wheat is ground through the mill.
Dough making	One part flour, one half-part warm water and about 1.4 per cent of dry yeast by weight of flour are mixed together, covered and left overnight to ferment.
	Add flour and warm water (four times original weight of flour and two times original weight of water).
	Mix well and knead for 5 minutes.
	Cover and leave to rest for 2 hours to let the dough rise.
	A small amount of fenugreek powder and salt can be added to the dough to improve the taste.
Moulding	Take half the dough and place in the middle of the working flat basket sprinkled with a little flour to prevent the dough from sticking. Pat with oiled palms into a circle about 1cm thick. Decorate by making several lines on the top of the dough using a fork or knife. Let it stand for a while until the *injera* oven (*metad*) gets warm.

Baking	Slide the dough from the basket onto the slightly greased *injera* oven, cover and bake for 10 minutes.
	Turn the bread over and bake for another 10 minutes.
	Bake the other half of the dough in the same way.

Process control

Wheat flour must be sifted with a fine sieve to remove bran and to produce soft and smooth textured *Ambasha*.

The starter must also be strong enough to ferment the dough to the desired level within the limited time.

Flour, water and starter should be in the right proportions to to produce a fermented *Ambasha* to the required texture.

The total fermentation period should not exceed 16 hours and after the dough is shaped, baking should be started.

Ambasha should be baked on both sides for no less than 10 minutes to produce the desired texture and colour.

Hygiene

Containers used to ferment the dough, storage basket and shaping basket must be cleaned well before each batch of *Ambasha* making.

Packaging and storage

Ambasha can be kept fresh for 2 days if it is covered with a plastic sheet or in a *messob* (a traditional straw basket with cover).

The formation of mould and drying out are the main problems and these can be minimized by storing *Ambasha* in cool and dry areas.

Rice bread and Quezadilla

Rice bread is a cake-like product and represents an attractive diversified use for rice. Quezadilla is a rice bread with cheese. It is a popular snack with a relatively good protein quality due to the cheese and eggs used.

Ingredients

2.7kg rice flour
908g sugar
454g butter
112g dried, salted cheese
9g baking powder
12 eggs (1 dozen)
½ litre cream

Equipment
Mixers
Moulds (cake tins)
Baking trays
Oven
Heat sealer (if polythene bags are used).

Process	Notes
Raw material	Rice flour, sugar, butter, cheese, eggs, baking powder and cream.
Mix	The sugar, butter and cream are mixed together and the cheese is sprinkled in.
Separate and mix	The egg whites and egg yolks are separated.
	The egg yolks and the rice flour are gradually added, mixing continuously.
	The egg whites are beaten until they look like snow and are stirred into the mixture little by little.
Baking	The mixture is put into a greased metal cake tin which has been lined with greaseproof paper and it is baked at 350°F (177°C) for 90 minutes.

Process control
All the ingredients should be weighed and measured to ensure the quality of the end product.

The times and temperature of the oven should be well controlled.

Hygiene
All the equipment used in the process should be clean.

Packaging and storage
Waxed paper and paper and polythene bags are most commonly used for packaging fresh rice bread. When it is sold, it is usually found in sealed polythene bags. When the product is transported, cardboard boxes are used to protect the loaves.

Injera

Injera is a traditional fermented bread. It is large, flat, round and uniformly thin and measures about 60cm in diameter. The top has uniformly spaced honeycomb-like eyes, each measuring about 4–5mm in diameter and the base has a smooth surface. *Injera* looks whitish cream, reddish brown or brown depending on the type of cereal flour used. It tastes slightly sour and is eaten with a kind of Ethiopian stew known as *wet*.

Equipment
Mortar and pestle
Winnowing basket
Traditional sieve
Metad
Stone mill

Process	Notes
Raw material	*Tef* is an indigenous cereal used for making *injera*. Other cereals which may be used are sorghum, millet, barley, wheat or a combination.
Cleaning	All impurities are removed by hand and winnowed in the case of sorghum, millet, barley and wheat.
	Tef is simply winnowed and sifted through a fine sieve.
Dehulling	Sorghum, barley and wheat are usually dampened and pounded, traditionally in a wooden mortar and pestle, to remove the bran.
	Mechanical hullers are also available.
Grinding	The sifted *tef* is ground through a flour mill.
Mix and first fermentation	Mix one part flour, two parts water and about 16 per cent *ersho* (a starter saved from previously fermented dough) by weight of the flour. Mix very well and leave to ferment for 3 days.
Thin and heat	Discard the surface water formed on top of the dough. For every 1kg of original flour, take about 200ml of the fermented mixture and add twice as

much water, mix and bring to the boil (tradition-ally this is called '*absit* making'). It should be cooled to about 115°F (46°C) before it is mixed into the main part of the dough. Thin the main dough by adding water equal to the original weight of the flour.

Batter making and second fermentation

Add the *absit* to the thinned dough and mix well to make batter. Leave the batter for about 30 minutes to rise before starting baking.

A small portion of the batter is saved to serve as a starter for the next batch.

Griddle

Injera is griddled by pouring about two thirds of a litre of the batter onto the hot greased electrical *metad* (*injera* griddle made of clay) using a circular motion from the outside towards the centre. It is cooked in about 2 to 3 minutes. Rapeseed oil is used to grease the *metad* between each one.

Store

Several layers of injera can be stored in a *messob* (traditional straw basket) with a tight cover for 3 days in a cool, dry, ventilated place.

Process control

Accurate weighing of ingredients and thorough mixing are both neces-sary to maintain the quality of the final product – the ratio of the flour, water and starch should be optimal to produce a fermented *injera* of the required taste. The *absit* should not be cooled below 115°F/46°C before it is mixed into the remainder dough in order to facilitate the second fermentation. Thorough mixing is required to obtain a uniform batter. The temperature of the *metad* should be hot enough so that each piece of *injera* is baked within 2-3 minutes, producing a uniformly soft – and unburnt *injera*.

Hygiene

Good hygiene practices should be carried out with respect to food handlers, raw materials, equipment and premises. The fermenting vat should be well cleaned after each batch of *injera* making. Potable water should be used. The *injera* must not be handled with wet hands as sur-face moisture will facilitate mould growth.

Packaging and storage

Good storage control is necessary to prevent mould growth which is a significant risk in this product. To prevent mould growth the product should be properly cooled and dry before packing as any surface moisture will encourage contamination. The straw baskets should have tight covers and be kept in a ventilated, cool, dry place, raised off the floor. Packaging also protects to some extent against insects, animals and soils.

Chapter 9
Other Bakery Products

Process control in cake- and biscuit-making

Advance preparation during any bakery process is essential and it is recommended that an adequate supply of paper-lined, greased cake tins or paper cup cases should be ready before the mixing starts.

Once again, the quality of the raw ingredients is important for an acceptable end product. Eggs should be fresh, without cracked or broken shells. Fresh milk and butter must be kept chilled prior to use. All dry ingredients should be stored in sealed containers to prevent infestation or contamination by pests. The flour must be free from foreign matter, soils and other contaminants, such as weevils.

Accurate weighing of all the ingredients is an important control point because small variations can cause significant differences in the final product.

During the beating of the batter, it is important that the inside of the mixing bowl is regularly scraped down to ensure a continuous distribution of the ingredients at an even viscosity level. Thorough mixing of all the ingredients will result in a uniform product.

The eggs should be given a short hand-whisk to break up and mix together the yolks and albumin. The eggs should be added to the batter in three or five equal portions ensuring that each portion has been fully incorporated before adding more eggs.

Temperature and time control of the cooking process are important to ensure the colour, texture and flavour qualities of the product.

Washing dried fruit – sultanas, currants and raisins

Dried fruit should be prewashed one or two days before being required for use. It should first be washed in clean, lukewarm water and rinsed twice. The fruit should then be immersed into boiling water for 30 seconds to 1 minute and rinsed in cold water before draining.

The drained fruit should be thinly spread over a large wooden tray lined with a clean, dry cloth and covered with a fine mesh net-cloth to protect it from flies. The fruit should be left to dry, preferably in a warm ambient temperature in a dust-free position, and turned over every three hours or so. Any stalks or small stones still present should be removed.

If dried fruit is being washed on a frequent basis, ensure that this is carried out in strict rotation to avoid any possible mould development.

During the washing process, the fruit will regain a degree of body fleshiness and will improve in eating quality. There will also be a gain in weight. Later, when the cake is sliced after baking, the cut fruit will glisten and be very attractive in appearance. The flavour of the cake will also be enhanced in taste and moistness.

Cake decoration

Water icing is used to decorate cakes. Icing sugar is sifted thoroughly to remove any lumps and water is added slowly while continually stirring (usually in the ratio of 1 part water to 11 parts icing sugar). Once the water has been incorporated, beat into a smooth mixture and either add more icing sugar or more water until the desired consistency has been obtained. Colours and/or flavours can be added but if these are in liquid form, an adjustment to the water will be required.

Hygiene

All utensils, cake tins etc. should be cleaned before use ensuring that the standard of hygiene is at a high level. As for breadmaking good hygienic practices should be carried out with respect to food handlers, raw materials, equipment and premises. Use potable water to avoid contamination.

Packaging and storage

Once again, good packaging and storage control are necessary to prevent mould growth. The product should be properly cooled before packing because surface moisture encourages contamination. Polythene bags and paper bags provide protection against some insects and soil contamination. The product should be stored in a ventilated, cool, dry place, raised off the floor.

Recipes for cakes and sweet bakery goods

All quantities for the ingredients are given for the production of a commercial batch.

Fermented doughnuts

Ingredients (60 doughnuts)

Ferment
230g bakers' strong flour
42g ordinary dried yeast –
weight of ordinary dried yeast
is calculated at 50 per cent that
of fresh yeast, therefore double
the quantities to arrive at the
amount of fresh yeast required.
21g granulated sugar
60g skimmed milk powder
1.135kg water

Dough
2.45kg bakers' strong flour
230g granulated sugar
230g bakers' fat/margarine
230g eggs
43g fine salt
Ferment

Additional ingredients
granulated sugar to roll the ingredients into
red-coloured jam/jelly to be injected into the centre of each doughnut.

Equipment
Dough mixer
Deep-fat fryer
Scales
Jam injector
Heat sealer (if polythene bags are used)

Process	Notes
Ferment	
Sift and mix	Sift the flour and the milk powder.
	Disperse the yeast and the sugar into 10 times its weight in water at a temperature of approximately 95°F (35°C) and set aside to activate for 12 minutes.
	Take the remainder of the water to a temperature of 95°F (35°C) and mix with the flour and milk powder.
	Immediately, add the activated yeast to obtain a thin liquid ferment and whisk vigorously for a few minutes.
Fermentation	Cover with a damp cloth and rest for 20 minutes.

Dough

Sift and mix	Sift the dough flour and mix with the granulated sugar. Then, rub in the fat.
	Disperse the salt into the eggs, whisk for about 1 minute then add to the dry ingredients, followed by the ferment. Mix together to obtain a soft dough.
Rest	The dough should rest for about 30 minutes covered by a damp cloth.
Knock-back	After resting, the dough is knocked-back, i.e. all the gas is expelled from the dough and it is kneaded slightly (1 minute of mixing with a machine will achieve this).
Roll form	Cover with a damp cloth and rest for 15 minutes.
	Divide the dough into equally weighed pieces (70g) and mould into balls or fingers approximately 9cm in length.
	Set the doughnuts approximately 2cm apart on a floured tray and cover with a warm damp cloth.
Final proof	Put into a steam space or cabinet for final proofing.
Deep fry	Cook in a deep hot fat, turning the doughnuts to obtain a golden brown all over.
Drain	When cooked, remove from fat and drain off.
Sugar coating	Roll the doughnuts in sugar while still warm.
Jam injection	Once cool, inject the ball doughnuts with jam. The finger doughnuts can be split and filled with fresh whipped cream or custard (see below).
Pack	Pack in paper or polythene bags depending on length of storage time before sale or consumption.

Custard filling
1kg milk
100g cornflour

155g sugar
195g egg yolks
flavouring (vanilla) as required
colouring (as required)

Use a little of the milk to make a paste with the cornflour and egg yolks.
Mix the sugar with the rest of the milk and bring to the boil.
Pour the boiling milk onto the cornflour, stirring rapidly to prevent the formation of lumps.
Return to the heat and bring to the boil, stirring continuously.
Add the flavourings and colouring if used.

Banana cake

Ingredients (8 cakes)
1kg bakers' fat/margarine
2kg granulated sugar
1kg eggs
2kg soft flour
31g baking powder
760g water
1.48kg mashed bananas

Equipment
Food mixer (optional)
Scales
Wire rack
Sieve
Greaseproof paper
Cake tins
Oven
Heat sealer/airtight containers

Process	Notes
Mix	Cream the margarine and sugar together until light and pale in colour.
	Lightly whisk the eggs and add to the batter in 3 equal portions, ensuring that each portion is fully incorporated into the batter before adding more eggs.

Sieve and fold	Sift and mix the flour and baking powder together. Gently fold into the batter.
Mix	Slowly mix in the water and rest for a few minutes.
	Add the bananas and mix in gently to obtain a smooth batter.
Fill	Line cake tins with a double greaseproof paper liner and fill with 1kg of batter. Spread level.
Bake	Bake in the oven at 350 to 360°F/177 to 182°C for 75 to 80 minutes.
Cool	Cool on a raised rack.
Decorate	The cakes can be lightly iced on top with water icing made up of 57–85g of icing sugar mixed with just sufficient water to make a stiffish icing.
Pack	Pack in an airtight container or seal in polythene bags depending on length of storage time before sale or consumption.

Eggless cake (fruited)

Ingredients (8 cakes)
1.82kg soft flour
115g baking powder
113g bicarbonate of soda
60g mixed spice
30g cinnamon
910g bakers' fat/margarine
910g granulated sugar
910g sultanas (prewashed and dried)
910g currants (prewashed and dried)
455g chopped peel
7g fine salt
1.59kg sour milk

Equipment
Food mixer (optional)
Scales
Wire rack
Sieve
Greaseproof paper
Cake tins
Oven
Heat sealer/airtight containers

Process	Notes
Sieve and mix	Sift and mix the flour, baking powder, bicarbonate of soda, spice and cinnamon together.
	Rub the fat into the dry ingredients.
Stir	Stir in the sultanas, currants, chopped peel and the sugar into flour mixture above.
	Dissolve the salt into the milk and add to the rest of the ingredients stirring quickly to give a smooth batter mixture.
Fill	Prepare cake tins by lining with double grease-proof paper and fill with 977g of cake mixture. Spread level.
Bake	Bake in an oven at 350°F/177°C for 1½ hours.
Cool	Cool on a raised rack.
Pack	Pack in an airtight container or seal in polythene bags depending on length of storage time before sale or consumption.

Spicy fruit cake

Ingredients (16 cakes)
1kg bakers' fat/margarine
1kg granulated sugar
480g eggs
1.24kg milk
31g fine salt
2kg soft flour
125g baking powder

62g mixed spice
30g cinnamon
1kg sultanas (prewashed and dried)
480g chopped nuts
240g mixed, chopped peel
480g chopped glacé cherries

Equipment
Food mixer (optional)
Scales
Wire rack
Sieve
Greaseproof paper
Cake tins
Oven
Heat sealer/airtight containers

Process	Notes
Mix	Cream the margarine and sugar together until light and pale in colour.
	Lightly whisk the eggs and add to the batter in 3 equal portions, ensuring that each portion is fully incorporated into the batter before adding more eggs. If there is any sign of the batter curdling, add a little flour to correct this.
Dissolve and stir	Dissolve the salt into the milk and gently stir half the milk into the batter.
Sieve and fold	Sift and mix the flour, baking powder and spice together. Gently fold into the batter. As the flour starts to become fully incorporated, add sufficient of the remaining milk to obtain a batter of dropping consistency.
Mix	Mix the sultanas, chopped nuts, peel and cherries together and gently fold and disperse evenly throughout the batter.
Fill	Line cake tins with a double greaseproof paper liner and fill with 500g of batter. Spread level and garnish on top of the unbaked cakes with a few chopped nuts and cherries.

Bake	Bake in the oven at 375°F/190°C for 50–60 minutes.
Cool	Cool on a raised rack.
Pack	Pack in an airtight container or seal in polythene bags depending on length of storage time before sale or consumption.

Assorted cup cakes

Ingredients (153 cakes)
1kg bakers' fat/margarine
1.24kg granulated sugar
1kg eggs
944g milk
31g fine salt
31g vanilla essence
2.24kg soft flour
93g baking powder

Equipment
Food mixer (optional)
Scales
Wire rack
Sieve
Baking trays and paper cups
Oven
Heat sealer/airtight containers

Process	**Notes**
Mix	Cream the margarine and sugar together until light and pale in colour.
	Lightly whisk the eggs and add to the batter in 3 equal portions, ensuring that each portion is fully incorporated into the batter before adding more eggs. If there is any sign of the batter curdling, add a little flour to correct this.
	Disperse the salt and the vanilla essence into the milk.

Sieve and fold	Sift and mix the flour and baking powder together.
	Add half the milk, stirring slowly into the batter.
	Add all the flour, gently folding into the batter. As the flour starts to become fully incorporated, add the remaining milk and gently beat for about 30 seconds to obtain a smooth batter.
Fill	Put small paper cups onto baking trays and, using a tablespoon, fill each one with 43g of batter. Once half the batter has been used, add sufficient cocoa powder to the remaining batter to make it chocolate and fill the cups as before.
Bake	Bake in the oven at 400°F/204°C for 16–18 minutes.
Cool	Cool on a raised rack.
Decorate	The cakes can be lightly iced on top with water icing made up of icing sugar mixed with just sufficient water to make a stiffish icing. A small piece of glacé cherry, half a cashew nut or a piece of flaked almond can be put onto the icing on each cake.
Pack	Pack in an airtight container or seal in polythene bags depending on length of storage time before sale or consumption.

Chocolate cakes

Ingredients (103 cakes)
760g bakers' fat/margarine
760g granulated sugar
480g eggs
1.24kg soft flour
62g baking powder
240g cocoa
880g milk

Equipment
Food mixer (optional)
Scales
Wire rack
Sieve
Baking trays and paper cups
Oven
Heat sealer/airtight containers

Process	Notes
Mix	Cream the margarine and sugar together until light and pale in colour.
	Lightly whisk the eggs and add to the batter in 3 equal portions, ensuring that each portion is fully incorporated into the batter before adding more eggs. If there is any sign of the batter curdling, add a little flour to correct this.
Sieve and fold	Sift and mix the flour, baking powder and cocoa together, and gently fold into the batter.
	Just as the flour starts to become fully incorporated, add the milk and gently beat for about 30 seconds to obtain a soft dropping consistency.
Fill	Put small paper cups onto baking trays and, using a tablespoon, fill each one with 43g of batter.
Bake	Bake in the oven at 375°F/190°C for 15–18 minutes.
Cool	Cool on a raised rack.
Decorate	The cakes can be lightly iced on top with either white water-icing made up of icing sugar mixed with just sufficient water to make a stiffish icing. A small piece of glacé cherry, half a cashew nut or a piece of flaked almond can be put onto the icing on each cake.
Pack	Pack in an airtight container or seal in polythene bags depending on length of storage time before sale or consumption.

Small coffee cakes

Ingredients (148 cakes)
2kg soft flour
125g baking powder
1kg bakers' fat/margarine
760g soft brown sugar
760g sultanas (prewashed and dried)
480g eggs
250g coffee essence
240g cocoa
1kg milk

Equipment
Food mixer (optional)
Scales
Wire rack
Sieve
Baking trays and paper cups
Oven
Heat sealer/airtight containers

Process	Notes
Sieve and mix	Sift and mix the flour and baking powder together, and rub the fat into the flour.
	Mix the sugar and sultanas into the flour mixture.
Whisk and stir	Whisk the egg and then stir in the coffee essence and three quarters of the milk. Add to the dry ingredients and mix together. Finally, add sufficient of the remaining milk to obtain a batter of dropping consistency.
Fill	Put small paper cups onto baking trays and, using a tablespoon or piping tube, fill each one with 43g of batter.
Bake	Bake in the oven at 400°F/204°C for 15–16 minutes.
Cool	Cool on a raised rack.

Decorate	When the cakes are cool, pipe a small spot of white icing onto the top of each cake and dip into desiccated coconut.
Pack	Pack in an airtight container or seal in polythene bags depending on length of storage time before sale or consumption.

Spicy nut cakes

Ingredients (143 cakes)
1kg bakers' fat/margarine
1kg granulated sugar
1kg eggs
2kg soft flour
30g baking powder
30g mixed spice
30g cinnamon
30g ground ginger
480g milk
480g finely chopped nuts

Equipment
Food mixer (optional)
Scales
Wire rack
Sieve
Baking trays and paper cups
Oven
Heat sealer/airtight containers

Process	Notes
Mix	Cream the margarine and sugar together until light and pale in colour.
	Stir the eggs together to break them up and then beat into the batter in 3 equal portions, ensuring that each portion is fully incorporated into the batter before adding more eggs.

Sieve and fold	Sift and mix the flour with the other dry ingredients.
	Gently fold into the batter adding the milk once the dry ingredients have been mixed in.
	Mix in about two thirds of the chopped nuts.
Fill	Put small paper cups onto baking trays and, using a tablespoon or piping tube, fill each one with 43g of batter.
	Sprinkle a few chopped nuts onto the top of each cake.
Bake	Bake in the oven at 380°F/193°C for 18–20 minutes.
Cool	Cool on a raised rack.
Pack	Pack in an airtight container or seal in polythene bags depending on length of storage time before sale or consumption.

Sponge cakes

Ingredients (8 cakes)
738g eggs
625g castor sugar
625g soft flour

Equipment
Food mixer (optional)
Scales
Wire rack
Sieve
Cake tins
Oven
Heat sealer/airtight containers

Process	Notes
Mix	Whisk the eggs and sugar together until fairly stiff.
Sieve and fold	Sift the flour and very gently fold into the sponge batter.

Grease and fill	Lightly grease 15 or 18cm diameter tins. Lightly dust the inside of each tin, first with flour and then with castor sugar shaking any surplus out of the tin on each occasion. Fill each tin with 240g of sponge batter.
Bake	Bake in the oven at 400°F/204°C for 16–18 minutes.
Cool	Cool on a raised rack.
Pack	Pack in an airtight container or seal in polythene bags depending on length of storage time before sale or consumption.

Featherlight ginger sponge

Ingredients (16 cakes)
455g arrowroot
455g soft flour
85g baking powder
57g cocoa
115g ground ginger
57g cinnamon
1.818kg eggs
455g granulated sugar
227g golden syrup

Equipment
Food mixer (optional)
Scales
Wire rack
Sieve
Cake tins
Oven
Heat sealer/airtight containers

Process	Notes
Sieve and fold	Sift and mix all the dry ingredients thoroughly together and set aside ready for use.
Separate and stir	Separate the egg whites from the yolks and whisk the whites stiff, adding the sugar gradually. Beat in the yolks in four equal portions.
Fold	Gently fold in the dry ingredients.

Heat and mix	Heat the golden syrup until runny and then mix in with the other ingredients.
Fill	Scale the batter into suitably sized greased tins (about 230g each).
Bake	Bake in the oven at 360°F/182°C for 30 to 35 minutes.
Cool	Cool on a raised rack.
Pack	Pack in an airtight container or seal in polythene bags depending on length of storage time before sale or consumption.

Nutty crisps

Ingredients (194 pieces)
1.48kg soft flour
40g bicarbonate of soda
1kg rolled oats
1kg crushed cashew nuts
2.48kg desiccated coconut
2.48kg granulated sugar
2kg bakers' fat/margarine
600g clear honey

Equipment
Food mixer
Cooking pan
Scales
Wire rack
Sieve
Baking trays
Oven
Heat sealer/airtight containers

Process	Notes
Mix	Sift and mix the flour and bicarbonate of soda and then mix with the rest of the dry ingredients.
Melt	Melt the fat and honey together using a low heat and mix into the dry ingredients to obtain a damp crumbly mixture.

Form	Heap the crumbly mixture into lightly greased, shallow patty pans (about 57g each). Press the mixture firmly down and push a cashew nut firmly into the centre of each.
Bake	Bake in the oven at 325°F/162°C until golden brown in appearance.
Cool	Cool on a raised rack.
Pack	Pack in an airtight container or seal in polythene bags depending on length of storage time before sale or consumption.

Currant scones

Ingredients (143 cakes)
455g bakers' fat/margarine
455g granulated sugar
455g eggs
28g fine salt
1.93kg liquid milk/sour milk
3.635kg soft flour
225g baking powder
680g currants (prewashed and dried)

Equipment
Dough mixer
Scales
Sieve
Baking trays
Oven
Heat sealer/airtight containers

Process	**Notes**
Mix	Cream the margarine and sugar together until light and pale in colour.
	Beat the eggs into the mixture in 3 equal portions, ensuring that each portion is fully incorporated into the batter before adding more eggs.

Dissolve	Dissolve the sugar into the milk and stir half the milk into the batter.
Sieve and mix	Sift and mix the flour and baking powder together.
	Add to the batter immediately following with the remainder of the milk.
	Add the currants and mix into a smooth soft dough.
Roll form	Divide the dough into 240g pieces and mould into ball shapes.
	Rest for a few minutes and roll out into circles about 13cm in diameter.
	Place suitably apart on lightly greased baking trays.
	Using a table scrapper dipped in vegetable oil or milk and divide into quarters.
	Neatly brush over the top of each circle of 4 scones with milk or egg glaze, or a light dust of flour.
	Alternatively, roll out the dough to 2cm thickness and cut out pieces of dough (about 56g) with a rounded flute cutter (diameter 6cm).
	Place on lightly greased baking trays and glaze with milk or dust with flour.
Bake	Bake in the oven between 400–420°F/204–215°C for 15 to 20 minutes.
Cool	Cool on a raised rack.
Pack	Pack in an airtight container or seal in polythene bags depending on length of storage time before sale or consumption.

Spiced scones

Ingredients (155 scones)
760g bakers' fat/margarine
760g granulated sugar
480g eggs
2kg milk
4kg soft flour
265g baking powder
80g mixed spice
1kg chopped mixed peel

Equipment
Dough mixer
Scales
Sieve
Baking trays
Oven
Heat sealer/airtight containers

Process	Notes
Mix	Cream the margarine and sugar together until light and pale in colour.
	Beat the eggs into the mixture in 3 equal portions, ensuring that each portion is fully incorporated into the batter before adding more eggs.
	Stir in the milk.
Sieve and mix	Sift and mix the flour and baking powder together.
	Mix the spice into the flour.
	Gently fold in the dry ingredients.
	Once the dry ingredients are almost fully incorporated, add the chopped peel and continue mixing gently to obtain a soft dough.
Roll form	Roll the dough into sausage shapes, approximately 4cm thick and cut into 60g pieces.
	Place suitably apart on lightly greased baking trays.

Neatly brush over the top of each scone with milk or egg glaze, and sprinkle with sugar.

Bake   Bake in the oven between 410°F/210°C for 18–20 minutes.

Cool   Cool on a raised rack.

Pack   Pack in an airtight container or seal in polythene bags depending on length of storage time before sale or consumption.

Almond slices

Ingredients (112 slices)

Base	*Filling*
1.825kg shortcrust pastry	545g egg whites
	1.135kg granulated sugar
	455g desiccated coconut
	455g flaked almonds
	1.345kg stoned dates

Equipment
Food mixer
Wire rack
Sieve
Baking trays
Oven
Cutters
Heat sealer/airtight containers

Process	**Notes**
Prepare baking tray	Line the baking tray (30″ × 18″ (approximately 76 × 46cm)) with shortcrust pastry.
	Place the dates evenly over the baking tray.
Whisk and mix	Whisk the egg whites for a few minutes to break them up.
	Mix in the sugar, desiccated coconut and flaked almonds until an even distribution has been obtained.

Fill	Pour the filling mixture over the top of the dates and spread evenly over the baking tray, ensuring that the dates are kept in the same place.
Bake	Bake in the oven between 360–380°F/182–193°C for 30 to 35 minutes.
Cool	Leave in the baking tray until thoroughly cool and then cut into slices measuring approximately 9.5 × 3cm.
Pack	Pack in an airtight container or seal in polythene bags depending on length of storage time before sale or consumption.

Date slices

Ingredients (112 pieces)

Base
1.825kg shortcrust pastry

Filling
1.12kg granulated sugar
895g desiccated coconut
225g ground almonds
455g egg whites
1.825kg stoned dates

Equipment
Food mixer
Wire rack
Sieve
Baking trays
Oven
Cutters
Heat sealer/airtight containers

Process	**Notes**
Prepare baking tray	Line the baking tray (30″ × 18″ (approximately 76 × 46cm)) with shortcrust pastry.
	Place the dates evenly over the baking tray.
Whisk and mix	Whisk the egg whites for a few minutes to break hem up.

Mix in the sugar, desiccated coconut and ground almonds until an even distribution has been obtained. If desired a few drops of yellow colour can be whisked in with the egg whites to enhance the appearance of the filling.

Fill	Pour the filling mixture over the top of the dates and spread evenly over the baking tray, ensuring that the dates are kept in the same place.
Bake	Bake in the oven between 360–380°F/182–193°C for 30 to 35 minutes.
Cool	Leave in the baking tray until thoroughly cool and then cut into slices measuring approximately 9.5 × 3cm.
Pack	Pack in an airtight container or seal in polythene bags depending on length of storage time before sale or consumption.

Fruit slices

Ingredients (112 pieces)

Base
3.64kg shortcrust pastry

Filling
1.37kg granulated sugar
1.45kg sultanas
1.45kg currants
370g stale cake-crumbs
370g water

Equipment
Food mixer
Wire rack
Sieve
Baking trays
Oven
Cutters
Heat sealer/airtight containers

Process	Notes
Prepare baking tray	Line the baking tray (30″ × 18″ (approximately 76 × 46 cm) with half the pastry, keeping aside the remainder for the top layer.
Mix	Mix the sugar, sultanas, currants, cake-crumbs and water together and spread evenly over the pastry base.
Roll out	Roll out the remaining half of the pastry to the shape of the baking tray (this should be the same thickness as the base).
	Lightly dust the pastry with flour and roll it round the rolling pin, unwinding it onto the top of the filling. When in position, give it a light roll to fix it to the filling.
Vent	Use a wide-pronged fork to create minute steam-vents while baking is taking place.
Bake	Bake in the oven between 360–375°F/182–190°C for 35–40 minutes. Approximately 5 minutes before baking is complete, remove the tray from the oven and lightly dust with sugar, then complete the baking until a light golden brown.
Cool	Leave in the baking tray until thoroughly cool and then cut into slices measuring approximately 9.5 × 3cm.
Pack	Pack in an airtight container or seal in polythene bags depending on length of storage time before sale or consumption.

Paradise slices

Ingredients (112 pieces)

Base
1.825kg shortcrust pastry

Filling
735g bakers' fat/margarine
735g granulated sugar
735g eggs

545g ground rice
355g ground almonds
195g soft flour
355g currants
285g sultanas
285g chopped cherries

Equipment
Food mixer
Wire rack
Sieve
Baking trays
Oven
Cutters
Heat sealer/airtight containers

Process	Notes
Prepare baking tray	Line the baking tray (30″ × 18″ (approximately 76 × 46cm)) with shortcrust pastry.
Beat	Beat the fat, sugar and eggs together until light and fluffy.
Sift and mix	Sift the flour and mix with the other dry ingredients. Gently fold into the batter.
	Mix the fruit together thoroughly and gently add into the batter until the fruit is evenly dispersed.
Fill	Pour the mixed filling onto the lined baking tray and spread level.
Bake	Bake in the oven between 360–380°F/182–193°C for 35–40 minutes. Just as the upper surface is becoming slightly coloured, remove from the oven and sprinkle a little sugar over the top and return to the oven. Cover with greaseproof paper if there is evidence of too much colouring on the upper surface.
Cool	Leave in the baking tray until thoroughly cool and then cut into slices weighing approximately 55g.

Pack	Pack in an airtight container or seal in polythene bags depending on length of storage time before sale or consumption.

Apple pies

Ingredients (10 pies)

Top and base
2.27kg shortcrust pastry

Filling
1.42kg chopped apples
285g granulated sugar
water (to moisten)

Equipment
Food mixer
Scales
Baking plates
Glazing brush
Oven
Heat sealer/airtight container

Process	**Notes**
Mix	Mix the chopped apples and sugar together with just sufficient water to moisten and keep ready for use.
Roll out	Scale the pastry into 114g pieces and mould into ball shapes. Flatten slightly and roll out to 20cm circles. Using 20cm diameter cardboard or tinfoil plates suitable for baking in the oven, line each plate with a circle of pastry.
Fill	Add 142g of chopped and sweetened apples and spread to within 1.5cm of the edge.
Cover	Moisten the circular edge with egg glaze and place the top circle of pastry directly over it. Close using slight finger pressure. Decoratively nick with a knife. Brush over the top with water and sprinkle a little sugar over the surface. Using a sharp knife incise a couple of air vents.

Bake	Bake in the oven between 375–400°F/190–204°C for 25–30 minutes.
Pack	Pack in an airtight container or seal in polythene bags depending on length of storage time before sale or consumption.

Coconut tarts

Ingredients (149 tarts)

Small tart base	*Filling*
4.4kg shortcrust pastry	375g egg whites
150g red jam	2.5kg granulated sugar
	1.55kg desiccated coconut

Equipment
Food mixer
Scales
Jam injector/piper
Baking tins
Oven
Heat sealer/airtight containers

Process	**Notes**
Prepare baking tins	Line small tart tins with approximately 28g of shortcrust pastry each.
Piping	Pipe a small amount of jam into the inside bottom of each lined tart tin.
Mix	Mix the egg whites, sugar and desiccated coconut into a wet mixture.
Fill	Deposit approximately 28g of mixture into each lined tart tin leaving a roughish appearance on the upper surface.
Bake	Bake in the oven between 360–380°F/182–193°C for 18–20 minutes.

Pack	Pack in an airtight container or seal in polythene bags depending on length of storage time before sale or consumption.

Small Bakewell tarts

Ingredients (72 tarts)

Bases
2.045kg shortcrust pastry
227g red jam

Filling
227g ground almonds
227g rice flour/sifted maizemeal
455g granulated sugar
228g bakers' fat/margarine
455g eggs
4g almond essence

Equipment
Food mixer
Scales
Rolling pin
Pastry cutter
Jam injector/piper
Baking tins
Oven
Heat sealer/airtight containers

Process	Notes
Roll out	Roll the pastry out to about ⅛ inch thickness and, using a round fluted cutter, cut out the bases and line sufficient shallow patty pans.
Piping	Pipe a good spot of red jam into the centre bottom of each and place on a baking tray. Keep ready for use.
Mix	Mix the ground almonds, rice flour and sugar together and then mix in the fat after melting it and stir together well.
	Add the egg with the essence mixed through and mix thoroughly with the other ingredients.
	If the mixture appears to be a little dry-mix in a teaspoonful of water and blend in.

Fill	Deposit approximately 21g of mixture into each patty pan.
Bake	Bake in the oven at 370°F/176°C for about 30 minutes.
Pack	Pack in an airtight container or seal in polythene bags depending on length of storage time before sale or consumption.

Cashew nut shorties

Ingredients
4kg bakers' fat/margarine
2.24kg granulated sugar
480g eggs
4.48kg soft flour
2kg finely ground cashew nuts

Equipment
Food mixer
Scales
Rolling pin
Pastry cutter
Baking trays
Glazing brush
Oven
Wire rack
Heat sealer/airtight containers

Process	Notes
Beat	Beat the margarine until light and creamy.
	Add the eggs and beat in, in 3 equal portions, scraping down the bowl on each occasion.
Sieve and mix	Sift the flour and mix in the ground cashew nuts then gently fold into the batter. Mix and knead to form a stiffish dough.
Roll out	Using as little dusting flour as possible, roll out part of the dough to approximately 0.6cm thickness and using a 5cm diameter circular cutter, cut out the dough (each piece weighing about 28g).

Lay out the biscuits about 2.5cm apart on a lightly greased baking tray.

Work the dough scraps from the first piece of dough into the second piece, and so on.

Glaze and garnish	Lightly glaze over the top of each biscuit with either a diluted egg glaze or milk. Garnish the top of each biscuit with a small piece of chopped cashew nut pressed into the centre.
Bake	Bake in the oven at 390–400°F/199–204°C for 12–15 minutes.
Cool	Cool on a raised rack.
Pack	Pack in an airtight container or seal in polythene bags depending on length of storage time before sale or consumption.

Coconut shorties

Ingredients (315 pieces)
4kg soft flour
120g baking powder
480g desiccated coconut
1.24kg bakers' fat/margarine
1.76kg granulated sugar
1.24kg eggs

Equipment
Food mixer
Scales
Rolling pin
Pastry cutter
Baking trays
Glazing brush
Oven
Wire rack
Heat sealer/airtight containers

Process	Notes
Sieve and mix	Sift and mix the flour and baking powder together. Mix in the desiccated coconut.
Rub in	Rub the fat into the dry ingredients until the mixture looks like bread crumbs.
Stir and mix	Stir the sugar and the eggs together and add to the dry ingredients, gently mixing and kneading together to obtain a stiffish dough.
Roll out	Using as little dusting flour as possible, roll out part of the dough to approximately 0.6cm thickness and using a 5cm diameter circular cutter, cut out the dough (each piece weighing about 28g). Lay out the biscuits about 2.5cm apart on a lightly greased baking tray. Work the dough scraps from the first piece of dough into the second piece and so on.
Glaze	Lightly glaze over the top of each biscuit with either a diluted egg glaze or milk, pricking each biscuit in the centre with a fork.
Bake	Bake in the oven at 400°F/204°C until golden brown on top. Be careful not to over-bake.
Cool	Cool on a raised rack.
Pack	Pack in an airtight container or seal in polythene bags depending on length of storage time before sale or consumption.

Crunchy currant crisps

Ingredients (158 pieces)
1kg bakers' fat/margarine
1kg granulated sugar
480g eggs
480g milk
1.24kg soft flour

240g currants (prewashed and dried)
vanilla essence as required

Equipment
Food mixer
Scales
Dough divider
Baking trays
Oven
Wire rack
Heat sealer/airtight containers

Process	Notes
Beat	Beat the margarine and sugar together until light and fluffy.
Mix	Stir the eggs, milk and vanilla essence together and gently mix in with the batter.
Sieve and fold	Sift the flour and mix in the currants.
	Gently fold into the batter to obtain a smooth dough.
Roll form	Divide the dough into 28g pieces and roll into balls (this can be done by a hand divider).
	Place the balls onto lightly greased baking trays about 3.5cm apart and using a flat surfaced object, press each ball out to 0.6cm thickness.
Bake	Bake in the oven at 360°F/182°C for 15–18 minutes until a pale brown colour.
Cool	Cool on a raised rack.
Pack	Pack in an airtight container or seal in polythene bags depending on length of storage time before sale or consumption.

Crunchy nutty crisps

Ingredients (150 pieces)
1kg bakers' fat/margarine
1kg granulated sugar
480g eggs
240g milk
1.24kg soft flour
240g chopped nuts

Equipment
Food mixer
Scales
Dough divider
Baking trays
Oven
Wire rack
Heat sealer/airtight containers

Process	Notes
Beat	Beat the margarine and sugar together until light and fluffy.
Mix	Stir the eggs and milk together and beat into the batter in 3 equal portions. Ensure that each portion is fully incorporated into the batter before adding more eggs/milk mixture.
Sieve and fold	Sift the flour and mix with the nuts.
	Gently fold into the batter to obtain a smooth soft dough.
Roll form	Divide the dough into 28g pieces and roll into balls (this can be done by a hand divider).
	Place the balls onto lightly greased baking trays about 3.5cm apart and using a flat surfaced object, press each ball out to 0.6cm thickness.
Bake	Bake in the oven at 350–360°F/177–182°C for 15–18 minutes until a pale brown colour.
Cool	Cool on a raised rack.

| Pack | Pack in an airtight container or seal in polythene bags depending on length of storage time before sale or consumption. |

Rough coconut biscuits

Ingredients (161 biscuits)
2.48kg soft flour
60g baking powder
880g bakers' fat/margarine
880g desiccated coconut
1.6kg granulated sugar
880g eggs

Equipment
Food mixer
Scales
Baking trays
Oven

Wire rack
Heat sealer/airtight containers

Process	Notes
Sieve and mix	Sift and mix the flour and baking powder together.
Rub in	Rub the fat into the dry ingredients until the mixture looks like bread-crumbs.
Mix	Mix in the desiccated coconut.
	Mix the sugar and the eggs together then add to the dry ingredients, gently mixing and kneading together to form a stiffish dough.
Roll out	Take a piece of the dough and roll out into a sausage shape approximately 3.5cm in diameter. Break into pieces weighing about 42g and place in rough heaps about 2.5cm apart on lightly greased baking trays.
Garnish	Garnish the centre of each biscuit with a small piece of glacé cherry or a piece of nut pressed into the centre of each one.

Bake	Bake in the oven at 400°F/204°C for about 15 minutes or until golden brown on top. Be careful not to overbake.
Cool	Cool on a raised rack.
Pack	Pack in an airtight container or seal in polythene bags depending on length of storage time before sale or consumption.

Appendices

Appendix 1: Temperature conversion table

Find the temperature to be converted in the *centre* column. Read off the *Celsius* conversion to the left and the *Fahrenheit* conversion to the right.

For example: 10.0 50 122.0 indicates that 50°C equals 122.0°F and that 50°F equals 10.0°C.

Deg. C		Deg. F	Deg. C		Deg. F	Deg. C		Deg. F
−17.8	0	32.0	7.2	45	113.0	32.2	90	194.0
−17.2	1	33.8	7.8	46	114.8	32.8	91	195.8
−16.7	2	35.6	8.3	47	116.6	33.3	92	197.6
−16.1	3	37.4	8.9	48	118.4	33.9	93	199.4
−15.6	4	39.2	9.4	49	120.2	34.4	94	201.2
−15.0	5	41.0	10.0	50	122.0	35.0	95	203.0
−14.4	6	42.8	10.6	51	123.8	35.6	96	204.8
−13.9	7	44.6	11.1	52	125.6	36.1	97	206.6
−13.3	8	46.4	11.7	53	127.4	36.7	98	208.4
−12.8	9	48.2	12.2	54	129.2	37.2	99	210.2
−12.2	10	50.0	12.8	55	131.0	37.8	100	212.0
−11.7	11	51.8	13.3	56	132.8	43.3	110	230.0
−11.1	12	53.6	13.9	57	134.6	48.9	120	248.0
−10.6	13	55.4	14.4	58	136.4	54.4	130	266.0
−10.0	14	57.2	15.0	59	138.2	60.0	140	284.0
− 9.4	15	59.0	15.6	60	140.0	65.6	150	302.0
− 8.9	16	60.8	16.1	61	141.8	71.1	160	320.0
− 8.3	17	62.6	16.7	62	143.6	76.7	170	338.0
− 7.8	18	64.4	17.2	63	145.4	82.2	180	356.0
− 7.2	19	66.2	17.8	64	147.2	87.8	190	374.0
− 6.7	20	68.0	18.3	65	149.0	93.3	200	392.0
− 6.1	21	69.8	18.9	66	150.8	98.9	210	410.0
−	−	−	−	−	−	100.0	212	413.6
− 5.6	22	71.6	19.4	67	152.6	104.4	220	428.0
− 5.0	23	73.4	20.0	68	154.4	110.0	230	446.0
− 4.4	24	75.2	20.6	69	156.2	115.6	240	464.0
− 3.9	25	77.0	21.1	70	158.0	121.1	250	482.0
− 3.3	26	78.8	21.7	71	159.8	126.7	260	500.0
− 2.8	27	80.6	22.2	72	161.6	132.2	270	518.0
− 2.2	28	82.4	22.8	73	163.4	137.8	280	536.0
− 1.7	29	84.2	23.3	74	165.2	143.3	290	554.0
− 1.1	30	86.0	23.9	75	167.0	148.9	300	572.0
− 0.6	31	87.8	24.4	76	168.8	154.4	310	590.0
0.0	32	89.6	25.0	77	170.6	160.0	320	608.0
0.6	33	91.4	25.6	78	172.4	165.6	330	626.0
1.1	34	93.2	26.1	79	174.2	171.1	340	644.0
1.7	35	95.0	26.7	80	176.0	176.7	350	662.0
2.2	36	96.8	27.2	81	177.8	182.2	360	680.0
2.8	37	98.6	27.8	82	179.6	187.8	370	698.0
3.3	38	100.4	28.3	83	181.4	193.3	380	716.0
3.9	39	102.2	28.9	84	183.2	198.9	390	734.0
4.4	40	104.0	29.4	85	185.0	204.4	400	752.0
5.0	41	105.8	30.0	86	186.8	218.3	425	797.0
5.6	42	107.6	30.6	87	188.6	232.2	450	842.0
6.1	43	109.4	31.1	88	190.4	246.1	475	887.0
6.7	44	111.2	31.7	89	192.2	260.0	500	932.0

Appendix 2: Weights and measures

Weight conversion – metric into imperial weight

1 kilogram equals 2.20462lbs
28.35 grams equals 1oz

Special note: Conversion of metric quantities to imperial does not give an exact conversion. The two systems of weights should not therefore be mixed.

Advice on weighing small quanities

Many domestic and commercial-type scales are not entirely suitable for weighing very small quantities of ingredients or additives, although it is possible to obtain scales suitable for this purpose through specialists in this field.

The following guide is given for certain ingredients commonly used in baking, and these recommendations will give a safe approximate measure of the quantity required.

While using this method I recommend that the reader either purchases a set of special graduated spoons, or uses domestic spoons – in which case the same spoons be used continuously if found to be suitable.

- *One level teaspoon of the following ingredients should give the equivalent of ⅛ of an ounce (say 3.5–4g)*

Baking powder	White or black pepper	Sugar
Bicarbonate of soda	All spices	
Cream of tartar	Fine dry salt	

- *One level dessertspoon of the following ingredient should give the equivalent of a ¼ of an ounce (say 7–8g)*

  Dried yeast

- *One heaped tablespoon of the following ingredients should give the equivalent of one ounce (say 28–30g)*

  Flour
  Ground almonds

- *Two heaped tablespoons of the following ingredients should give the equivalent of one ounce (say 28–30g)*

  Arrowroot
  Dried breadcrumbs
  Fresh breadcrumbs

Eggs

Eggs should be shelled and weighed in the same way as any other ingredients. Where the recipe stipulates whole eggs, it helps with the inclusion if the eggs are given a quick whisk to break them up before adding to the other ingredients (e.g. in cake-making).

Throughout the book the following classifications are used with respect to different egg sizes.

Large eggs   – not less than 62g (2³⁄₁₆ ozs)
Standard eggs   – between 53.25–62g (1⅞ to 2³⁄₁₆ ozs)
Medium eggs   – between 46–53.25g (1⅝ to 1⅞ ozs)
Small eggs   – between 42.6–46g (1½ to 1⅝ ozs)
Extra-small eggs   – under 42.6g (1½ ozs)

Appendix 3: Oven temperatures and related hints

In developing countries, one can find a very wide range of differing ovens, from the locally made oven (often lacking a thermometer) to the plant unit equipped with a tunnel-type travelling oven.

Without a thermometer, an oven is like a ship without a compass, and my very strong recommendation is that owners of ovens without thermometers should really have one fitted to each baking chamber.

As a guide to oven temperature control I list the following data on the subject (indicating the varying categories of heat) which has been extended to include domestic gas and electric ovens and gives an approximate guidance to the regulo settings.

deg. F.	deg. C	Descriptive category	Approx. gas regulo setting	Approx. elec. regulo setting
250–275	121–135	Very cool oven	3–5	½–1
275–310	135–154	Cool oven	6	2
310–330	154–166	Warm or slow oven	7	3
330–375	166–191	Moderate oven	8	4
375–420	191–216	Fairly hot oven	9	5–6
420–450	216–232	Hot oven	10	7
450–500	232–260	Very hot oven	11	8–9

In general the following hints may prove helpful:

o It is possible with certain types of ovens (e.g. oil or electric-fired) to bake 'short baking time' products on rising heat, and with 'cooling' oven, on 'dropping' heat.

○ Usually, oven heat is raised to the highest temperature required and products are baked on a dropping heat situation (i.e. once the high-baking-temperature products have been baked, then products requiring less heat are baked and so on, thereby using the heat productivity of the oven as economically as possible.

○ A continuity of the baking chamber being kept at full capacity will serve to obtain a continuing similarity in baked quality.

○ In the instance of a travelling oven where there is an end of a particular product throughput, creating an oven space in the throughput (to overcome the effect of any 'flash heat') a row of old sand-filled bread tins should be placed immediately behind the last row of the end of a product run, and again immediately in front of the first row of the new run of products.

Appendix 4: Building a de-panning table

The de-panning table in Figure A.1 is suitable for de-panning bread direct from wheeled racks being used for the rack oven.

The de-panning table in Figure A.3 is suitable for de-panning bread straight from a travelling oven. Except for the table-top area, the measurements for the table legs and wood thickness are exactly the same as for the smaller table. The rubber tapping-out bar is also the same type of rubber sheeting and thickness, the length of the tapping-out bar for the larger table being 3m. The purpose of the tapping-out bar

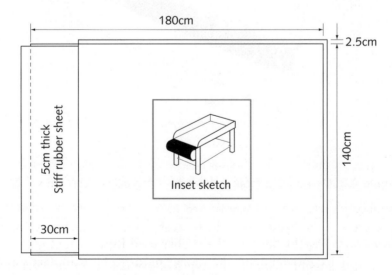

Figure A.1: The plan view of a table-top area of 180cm x 140cm

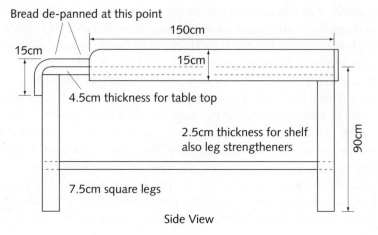

Figure A.2: The side view of a de-panning table suitable for a travelling oven

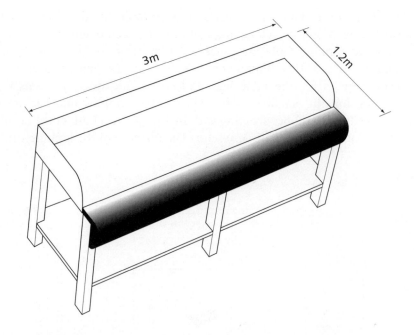

Figure A.3: De-panning table suitable for a travelling oven 3m x 1.2m

is to prevent tin distortion in the process of tapping the bread out of the bread tins. The thickness of the rubber used for the tapping-out bar is of a similar consistency to the rubber used in the manufacture of car tyres.

It is very important that the packers handling the de-panned bread protect their hands with clean handling gloves in order that the hot bread is kept clean and undamaged through rough handling. The oven strippers who actually tap the bread out of the tins must not handle the de-panned bread with greasy or stained oven gloves.

Bibliography

Traditional Foods: Processing for profit, P. Fellows (Editor), 1996, IT Publications, 103–105 Southampton Row, London, WC1B 4HH, UK. (ISBN 1 85339 228 6)

Starting a Small Food Processing Enterprise, P. Fellows, E. Franco and W. Rios, 1996, IT Publications (address above). (ISBN 1 85339 323 1)

Small-scale Food Processing: A guide to appropriate equipment, P. Fellows and A. Hampton, 1992, IT Publications (address above). (ISBN 1 85339 108 5)

Food Cycle Technology Source Books, series aimed at women covering various aspects of food processing, IT Publications (address above).

Making Safe Food, P. Fellows, V. Hidellage and E. Judge, 1998, from ITDG, The Schumacher Centre for Technology and Development, Bourton Hall, Bourton on Dunsmore, Rugby, Warwickshire, CV23 9QZ, UK.

Appropriate Food Packaging, P. Fellows and B. Axtell, 1993, TOOL Publications, (ISBN 90 70857 28 6)

Bakery – Flour Confectionery, L.J. Hanneman, 1991, Butterworth-Heinemann Ltd., Linacre House, Jordan Hill, Oxford, OX2 8DP, UK. (ISBN 0 7506 0447 6)

Bakery – Bread and Fermented Goods, L.J. Hanneman, 1987, Butterworth-Heinemann Ltd., Linacre House, Jordan Hill, Oxford, OX2 8DP, UK. (ISBN 0 434 90708 1)